THE MSP G

ENDORSEMENTS

"...Multi-stakeholder partnerships are, although not the easiest, certainly the most effective way forward to make sure no one is left behind when taking decisions that affect us all. I am struck by the amount of experience and quality of insight gathered in this guide, which echo many situations we encounter at the UN Committee on World Food Security (CFS) throughout our continuing learning journey to ensure inclusive policies for zero hunger and malnutrition." - **Gerda Verburg, Chair of the UN Committee on World Food Security (CFS)**

"...'The MSP Guide' is a welcome and invaluable management tool for identifying the core principles, tools and considerations needed to optimise your organisation's approach to engagement..." - **Paul Hohnen, Sustainability Strategies, Amsterdam, and Associate Fellow, Chatham House**

"What I like about this manual – and I like it a lot – is the way the authors have drawn on a rich tapestry of global experience and wide range of professional disciplines to enable those who read it to tackle the innumerable challenges of collaboration with increased confidence and competence." - **Ros Tennyson, Partnership Brokers Association**

"It is truly wonderful to see this Guide that draws from such deep experience and range of sources in a presentation that is comprehensive and easily accessible for those creating MSPs." - **Steve Waddell, Principal - NetworkingAction, author of Global Action Networks: Creating our future together**

"Managing multi-stakeholder partnerships is both an art and a science. This guide offers both practical guidance and unique insights drawn from real experience, providing the most comprehensive resource available on the subject." - **Lisa Dreier, Head of Food Security and Agriculture Initiatives, World Economic Forum USA**

THE MSP GUIDE

HOW TO DESIGN AND FACILITATE MULTI-STAKEHOLDER PARTNERSHIPS

Herman Brouwer and Jim Woodhill
with Minu Hemmati, Karèn Verhoosel
and Simone van Vugt

PRACTICAL ACTION
Publishing

Practical Action Publishing Ltd
The Schumacher Centre, Bourton on Dunsmore,
Rugby, Warwickshire, CV23 9QZ, UK
www.practicalactionpublishing.org

Centre for Development Innovation,
PO Box 88, 6700 AB Wageningen,
The Netherlands
www.wageningenUR.nl.cdi

First edition published by
Centre for Development Innovation,
Wageningen University and Research, 2015
This edition published by
Practical Action Publishing Ltd, 2016

A catalogue record for this book is available from
the British Library.
A catalogue record for this book has been
requested from the Library of Congress.

ISBN 978-1-85339-965-7 Paperback
ISBN 978-1-78044-669-1 Library Ebook
ISBN 978-1-78044-965-4 Ebook

Citation: Brouwer, Herman and Woodhill, Jim,
with Hemmati, Minu, Verhoosel, Karèn
and van Vugt, Simone (2016) The MSP Guide,
How to design and facilitate multi-stakeholder
partnerships, Wageningen:
Wageningen University and Research, CDI,
and Rugby, UK: Practical Action Publishing,
http://dx.doi.org/10.3362/9781780446691

Since 1974, Practical Action Publishing has
published and disseminated books and
information in support of international
development work throughout the world.
Practical Action Publishing is a trading name
of Practical Action Publishing Ltd (Company
Reg. No. 1159018), the wholly owned publishing
company of Practical Action. Practical Action
Publishing trades only in support of its parent
charity objectives and any profits are covenanted
back to Practical Action (Charity Reg. No. 247257,
Group VAT Registration No. 880 9924 76).

The Centre for Development Innovation (CDI) of
Wageningen UR focuses on the global challenges
of secure and healthy food, sustainable markets,
adaptive agriculture, ecosystem governance,
and conflict and reconstruction. We link cutting
edge processes of innovation and learning
with Wageningen UR's world-leading scientific
and technical expertise. We work with farmers
and NGOs, businesses and entrepreneurs, and
governments and international organisations in
many different countries to support and facilitate
processes of innovation and change.

Design: Roger Reuver and Paulien Hassink
www.reuverandco.com

THANK YOU

CDI co-workers: Fannie de Boer, Diane Bosch, Marleen Brouwer, Jan Brouwers, Toon de Bruyn, Karen Buchanan, Alberto Giani, Femke Gordijn, Annemarie Groot Kormelinck, Joost Guijt, Karen de Hauwere, Jan Helder, Melike Hemmami, Riti Herman Mostert, Wouterleen Hijweege, Ton Hoogveldt, Annette van 't Hull, Dieuwke Klaver, Irene Koomen, Esther Koopmanschap, Cecile Kusters, Jan van der Lee, James Mulkerrins, Cora van Oosten, Siri Pisters, Nina de Roo, Nico Rozemeijer, Mirjam Schaap, Monika Sopov, Seerp Wigboldus, Henk Zingstra

Others: Noelle Aarts, Wageningen UR | Hilary Asiah | Simon Bachelor, Gamos | Karen Batjes | Domenico Dentoni, Wageningen UR | Art Dewulf, Wageningen UR | Priska Dittrich | Willem Elbers, Radboud University | Louise O. Fresco, Wageningen UR | Kathy Hurly, Canegrowers | Wijnand van IJssel, DGIS | Jouwert van Geene, The Hunger Project | Ken Giller, Wageningen UR | Christopher Gohl | Irene Guijt, Learning by Design | Kate Hamilton | Wim Hiemstra, ETC | Thea Hilhorst, KIT | Surinder Hundal, PBA | Ulrich Klins, Southern Africa Trust | Rina Kusuma, Ewen Leborgne, ILRI and KM4Dev | Cees Leeuwis, Wageningen UR | Penpen Libres | Frank Mechielsen, OxfamNovib | Thembinkosi Mhlongo, SADC | Mike Morris, WWF-UK | Jethro Pettit, IDS | Kavita Prakash-Mani, Grow Asia | Smita Premchander, Sampark | Citra Presetyawati | Bettye Pruitt, D3Associates | Rina Puspitasari | Henk Reitsema | Iñigo Retolaza | Pier Paolo Roggeri, University of Sassari | Niels Röling | Bert Ronhaar, Special Envoy of the Netherlands to Nigeria | Puvan Selvanathan, UN Global Compact | Roel Snelder, AgriProfocus | Thandokwakhe Sibiya, Canegrowers | Dave Snowden, Cognitive Edge | Mark Spain, Global Learning | Kesaraporn Sreechun, Ros Tennyson, PBA | Philip Thomas, D3Associates | Jan Ubels, SNV | Steve Waddell, Networkingaction | Marieke de Wal, Partnerships Resource Centre | Arjen Wals, Wageningen UR | Hettie Walters, ICCO | Jeroen Warner, Wageningen UR | Diana Widiastuti | all AMID trainees 2011 to 2015 at Radboud University Nijmegen | all presenters and participants of CDI Seminars related to MSP in the past decade | all MSP course participants 2003 to 2016 at CDI Wageningen UR |

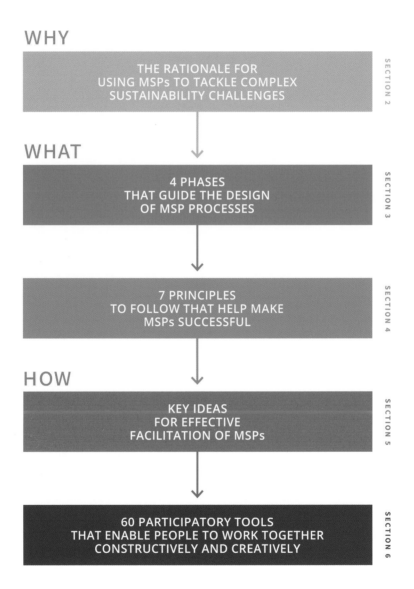

WHY

THE RATIONALE FOR
USING MSPs TO TACKLE COMPLEX
SUSTAINABILITY CHALLENGES

SECTION 2

WHAT

4 PHASES
THAT GUIDE THE DESIGN
OF MSP PROCESSES

SECTION 3

7 PRINCIPLES
TO FOLLOW THAT HELP MAKE
MSPs SUCCESSFUL

SECTION 4

HOW

KEY IDEAS
FOR EFFECTIVE
FACILITATION OF MSPs

SECTION 5

60 PARTICIPATORY TOOLS
THAT ENABLE PEOPLE TO WORK TOGETHER
CONSTRUCTIVELY AND CREATIVELY

SECTION 6

THE AUTHORS

Herman Brouwer (MA) is a multi-stakeholder engagement specialist working at CDI, Wageningen UR. He advises, trains and coaches professionals across sectoral boundaries on how to contribute to sustainable development through collaboration. As an accredited PBA partnership broker, Herman is supporting local and global MSPs, mainly in food security and natural resource management.

Jim Woodhill (PhD) is the former Director of CDI at Wageningen UR and former Principal Sector Specialist for Food Security and Rural Development at the Australian Department of Foreign Affairs and Trade. He is an independent consultant on food systems, inclusive agribusiness and MSPs. Jim's understanding of applying systems thinking and participatory learning to complex issues is gained from his experience as a process facilitator working in sustainable development across the boundaries of business, government, civil society and science.

Dr. Minu Hemmati is a psychologist working independently in practice, advocacy, training and research of designing, facilitating and coaching multi-stakeholder processes for sustainability and gender justice. Minu has experience with MSPs at all levels; international policy-making on sustainable development and related issues; local and national level implementation and evaluation. www.minuhemmati.net

Karèn Verhoosel (MA) works at CDI, Wageningen UR as an advisor on facilitation of multi stakeholder processes, institutional change, monitoring and evaluation and capacity development. She has experience as process facilitator working in fields of integrated seed sector development (ISSD), agribusiness and food and nutrition security.

Simone van Vugt (MSc) is a socio economist working at CDI, Wageningen UR facilitating multi-stakeholder processes in value chain programmes and integrated food security and sector development programmes. Simone conducts action research and training on MSPs, and has experience with the development of Planning Monitoring & Evaluation systems within MSPs.

Welcome to this guide on facilitating Multi-Stakeholder Partnerships (MSPs).

For more than a decade, the Centre for Development Innovation (CDI) has been running an annual three-week international course on facilitating MSPs and social learning. This course evolved from the diverse experience of CDI staff in initiating, facilitating, and participating in multi-stakeholder partnerships in many parts of the world. Over the years, the course has been refined based on insights and feedback from hundreds of course participants. Versions of the course have also been tailor-made for numerous clients across business, government, and civil society. The guide distils this wealth of experience for a wider audience.

Today's complex and interconnected world clearly needs collaboration and partnerships between interest groups spanning the boundaries of business, government, civil society, and science. But bringing about such collaboration is no simple matter. It requires deep understanding of what enables and what stops people from working together. It requires patience, time, and commitment from leaders. However, with the right mindset, and by using the practical process steps and tools offered in this guide, much can be done to unlock people's potential to cooperate and innovate for social and environmental good.

The guide integrates practical knowledge with theoretical foundations and principles. While practical facilitation methods and tools are essential, it is even more important to be able to design processes around the underlying dynamics of human systems, power relations, conflict, and teamwork. We draw on diverse schools of thought to offer facilitators and stakeholders in partnerships a set of principles and conceptual models to help inspire creative and critical processes of change.

Our approach to MSPs has strong roots in participatory development, which has become a cornerstone of effective development cooperation. Participatory development grew from participatory rural appraisal (PRA). This work pioneered the use of creative and visual methods for local communities to manage their own development. These approaches have inspired work at a larger scale, as in regional and global value chains and environmental issues. Methodological innovation in civil society, government, and the private sector has also inspired those working in 'design thinking' and 'social innovation labs'. While these developments are promising, there are still many examples of missed opportunities. Poorly designed and poorly facilitated collaborative projects are common; the people involved do not always know what is needed to make them work well. We hope that this guide will help provide practical insights to make collaborative work inspiring, effective and fun.

1 INTRODUCTION

Are you working to connect businesses and NGOs to create better environmental and social standards? Or are you a government policy officer needing to work with the fisheries sector and local communities to create a sustainable management plan? Is your business partnering with farmer organisations, NGOs, and an impact investor to source responsibly from small-scale farmers? Perhaps your NGO is trying to work with government and businesses to create more opportunities for youth in rural areas?

Multi-stakeholder partnerships offer practical ways forward in these types of situations, and in many others. How to design, facilitate and manage these partnerships is what this book is all about.

In 2015 the global community agreed to a set of Sustainable Development Goals that address the big issues facing humanity for the coming decades. They will only be achieved through strengthened multi-stakeholder partnerships, as the UN Secretary General himself recognises. It will be the collective efforts of partnerships everywhere that will make the difference. This guide is a contribution to that effort.

PEOPLE

PLANET

PROFIT

CIVIL
SOCIETY

GOVERNMENT

BUSINESS

SCIENCE

*MSPs: collaborating
to tackle the complexity of
sustainable development*

MSPs are advocated by everyone

Paul Polman
CEO of Unilever

"The issues we face are so big and the targets are so challenging that we cannot do it alone. When you look at any issue, such as food or water scarcity, it is very clear that no individual institution, government, or company can provide the solution."

Ban Ki-Moon
UN Secretary General

"One of the main lessons I have learned during my five years as Secretary-General is that broad partnerships are the key to solving broad challenges. When governments, the United Nations, businesses, philanthropies, and civil society work hand-in-hand, we can achieve great things."

Neil Keny-Guyer
CEO of Mercy Corps

"We live in a time where the boundaries between the public, private, and civil silos are blurring and breaking down. If we are going to find solutions to poverty and injustice, it is going to be in that blurred space, not in the silo space."

Louise O. Fresco
President of Wageningen UR

"While better methods to produce scientific and technical knowledge remain necessary, they need to be integrated with methods that produce practical wisdom to guide us in our strategies and actions in a moral, ethical, and political rather than only in a technical and instrumental sense."

The challenges of our globalised world

We are living in a globalised world with a population heading towards nine billion people, putting the earth's resources under immense pressure. Increasingly, we find that the challenges and opportunities we face are large and complex. Our actions are linked with the actions of others, our solutions are embedded in a web of interlinked interests and responses, and we cannot work alone. There is a profound need for new approaches – for innovation – in how we govern ourselves, in how we use and share resources, and in how we create harmony between people of differing wealth, culture, and religion.

Creating a better world takes partnership. Increasingly, government, business, civil society, and science recognise the need to work together to tackle the challenges of the modern world and bring about change for the common good. Many of the issues we confront and the opportunities we would like to exploit are embedded in a network of changing social, economic, political, and environmental factors. And many different groups may be concerned with the same issues, but from a different perspective and with different interests. In our world of social media and interconnected economies, bringing about change depends on dialogue and alignment across different sectors in society. We need to foster relationships across these groups and help them collaborate. Although no one group can bring about change on its own, the power of one group can be enough to block the actions of others. To avoid this, we need to develop shared perspectives, new understanding, and collective commitment for action, even between groups who may at first seem to have diverging interests or be in conflict.

Partnering for change

If you want to tackle real world issues and achieve real change, you will need to work together with a range of different people and organisations with different backgrounds. This is what we mean by a 'multi-stakeholder partnership' (MSP). While the different actors may share a common problem or aspiration, they also have different 'stakes' or interests. Across the world, people are creating new coalitions, alliances, and partnerships, and many inspirational examples are emerging of what can be achieved when people mobilise to take action together. But just agreeing to work together is no guarantee of success. The way these partnerships are set up, the process taken, the capacity for leadership, and the skill of facilitation will have a strong impact on how they develop and how successful they are. Enabling people to work well together, especially if they start with very different views of the world or are in conflict, is never easy. But if you succeed you will be able to make the most of the potential for human good, innovation, and transformational change.

The good news is that from experience we now know much more about how to create successful partnerships for change through multi-stakeholder collaboration. And, as successful examples gain attention, business, government, and non-governmental organisation (NGO) leaders are increasingly calling for more. This wave has been called 'the collaboration paradigm of the 21st century'[1] and a 'stunning evolutionary change in institutional forms of governance'.[2] Civil society organisations have discovered that they are more effective if they engage and collaborate.[3] Citizens discover that they can change their world by finding new ways to collaborate and make demands using online tools. And business is looking to new ways that bring 'shared value'.[4]

The collaborative and learning-oriented approach of MSPs is certainly not a silver bullet for every difficult situation we face. Yet, it is often surprising just how much progress can be made when you focus on the human aspects that help people cooperate, rather than remaining locked in conflict.

This guide aims to:

- be a backup for professionals involved in MSPs,
- inspire readers to try out new approaches for facilitation,
- connect to the theory that underpins MSP practice, and
- point readers to practical tools that can make their MSP practice more effective and rewarding

Is this guide for you?

This guide is for anyone interested in MSPs and how to make them more effective. It is particularly addressed to anyone responsible for setting up, leading, or facilitating an MSP – the 'you' of this book – but will be equally useful for those involved in commissioning, funding, or managing an MSP, and even for those who would just like to know what MSPs are about. If you are interested in combining practical steps and tools with a deeper insight into the theoretical foundations and underlying principles of MSPs, you will find the guide especially useful. And we hope it will also be a valuable resource for training in MSP and facilitation skills, as well as for use in higher education courses.

The guide offers a roadmap for designing and facilitating MSPs. We have woven together real world experience with sound theoretical foundations and practical facilitation tools to provide a coherent approach for getting the best out of an MSP. This is not a recipe book; rather, it provides a broad outline. Each MSP will have its own unique dynamics requiring insight and creativity to bring out the best in people and to forge the understanding and collaborative relationships that make change possible. We have written this guide to help you bring insight and creativity to the process of your MSP.

Like us, you may be familiar with MSPs that start full of energy and a spirit of optimism, but where the enthusiasm slowly but surely fades away. Some people become impatient and leave. Others start doubting that the MSP can deliver real change, or they feel unheard. Establishing an MSP doesn't automatically lead to harmonious collaboration between the partners. You may need a lot of patience. Developing trust and understanding can be a slow and difficult process when people have opposing interests or are competing for resources, or there are deep or long-held conflicts. It may take time until all partners understand and agree on the need for shared decisions and collective action. The guide will give you ideas and strategies for working through such challenges.

Our experiences of MSPs come largely from the agriculture, food and natural resource managements sectors, and the examples we use are drawn mostly from this work. However, the basic framework for MSPs that we offer is not sector specific so it will be just as relevant for working in other sectors such as health, education, governance, economic development, peace building or community development.

We hope that the guide will help committed businesses, governments, NGOs, and researchers to become more effective in their efforts to achieve environmental and economic sustainability and social justice. Each of these groups will come to an MSP with different interests, values, responsibilities, technical language, communication styles, and constraints. We have tried to ensure that this guide speaks to the needs of all.

How to use the guide

The power of this guide comes from its underlying framework for understanding and facilitating MSPs. This framework links theory with practice and provides a model and set of principles to guide the design of MSPs, tips on facilitation, and a set of participatory process tools.

The guide has been designed so that you can dip in at different places to find what you need, without reading cover to cover. In Section 2, we discuss MSPs in more detail, what they are, and their key characteristics. Section 3 focuses on the key elements for developing an MSP, the different phases, and designing the MSP process. Section 4 looks at seven principles that we have identified as the basis for effective MSPs, backed up by a set of conceptual models that capture key theoretical ideas and will help you to understand how MSPs can make transformative change possible. Section 5 looks at moving from design to practice – what it takes to facilitate an MSP and support partnership processes, what human dimensions need to be in place, and how you get organised. Section 6 considers the type of tools you will need at different stages of the MSP process, and gives a brief introduction to a selection of participatory tools that can be used to help stakeholders work more effectively together in building trust, exploring issues, strategising, and planning action. Section 7 offers you some stories from the frontline in the form of interviews with different stakeholders talking about their experience with MSPs. Finally, a resources section gives you links to further information on the theoretical basis of MSP practice, details of the references, and additional resources.

The guide is backed up by the CDI MSP resource portal (www.mspguide. org), where you will also find more details on the underlying theory of MSPs, additional examples and case studies, detailed descriptions of the tools, and many other resources.

Finally

Remember, the primary 'tool' at your disposal is... yourself. We assume that you have picked up this guide because you want to change something, and have realised that you will need to do this together with others. The quality of your personal leadership to drive change is more than the sum of all the tools and concepts in this guide. It is also about integrity, knowing yourself, balancing the head and the heart. This guide can help you hone your ability to become a more effective change agent. We have included reflection questions to help you on this path.

Some questions this guide will help you answer:

- **Stakeholder identification:** Who are the main stakeholders, and how do we know the right ones are involved?
- **Power:** How can we deal with power differences?
- **Common goal:** How can we define a common goal among diverse stakeholders? Should there be one?
- **Governance structure:** How do we organise our collaboration and decision making?
- **Conflict:** How do we deal with conflicts among stakeholders?
- **Capacity:** What can we do if essential stakeholders lack the capacity to lead and deliver?
- **Efficiency:** In which situations are MSPs not the right choice?
- **Tools:** What tools are available for helping the MSP achieve its goals?
- **Facilitation:** Who should facilitate an MSP: one person, a group? From within the system or an outside professional?

2 MULTI-STAKEHOLDER PARTNERSHIPS

We can understand that the best way to address complex issues is for the different groups affected – the stakeholders – to work together in partnership. But what does this actually mean? Are there different types of partnership, do they have different purposes, what are their common characteristics? And what is a 'stakeholder'? How does the process work? This section looks at how we can define multi-stakeholder partnerships or MSPs, how such partnerships work, and how we can judge whether an MSP is the best choice for our issue.

Multi-stakeholder partnerships

Global Action Network

Multi-actor platforms

Innovation Platform

Hosting

Cross-sector partnership

Roundtable

Multi-stakeholder initiative

Social Learning

Knowledge co-creation

Stakeholder dialogues

Learning Alliance

Multi-stakeholder processes

Participatory planning

Boundary spanning

System innovation

Social Lab

Collaborative action

Interactive Policy Making

Cross-industry collaboration

Collective impact

*Terms often used
to describe
multi-stakeholder
partnerships*

What are Multi-Stakeholder Partnerships?

There are many different ways for groups to work together to solve a large and complex problem, or exploit a promising new opportunity. And people use many different words to describe these types of partnerships and interactions and the processes involved, from coalitions, alliances, and platforms, to participatory governance, stakeholder engagement, and interactive policy-making. We use the term 'multi-stakeholder partnership' (MSP) as an overarching concept which highlights the idea that different groups can share a common problem or aspiration, while nonetheless having different interests or 'stakes'.

At CDI, we see MSPs as a form of governance – in other words, a way in which groups of people can make decisions and take action for the collective good, be it at local, national, or international scale. A central part of our vision is the role of MSPs as a platform where stakeholders can learn together in an interactive way, where people can speak and be heard, and where everybody's ideas can be harnessed to drive innovation and find ways forward that are more likely to be in the interests of all.

MSPs range from short consultation processes through to multi-year engagements that may evolve through many phases. Some MSPs may be very structured and backed by formal organisational arrangements. Others may be much more ad hoc and fluid. Different groups will take the lead in initiating MSPs. Governments may initiate a stakeholder consultation process for assessing new policy directions. NGOs may work to bring business and government together around an environmental or social concern. Business may realise they need to partner with government and NGOs to create new market opportunities and to manage their operations in ways that create shared value and give them a 'licence to operate'.

Thousands of examples of MSPs have emerged over the last decade. Take the global food and beverage sector, where twenty-two of the world's largest multi-national corporations have joined in partnerships with stakeholders from the public sector and civil society.[5] Or the hundreds of partnerships formed by development organisations, government, and civil society following the World Summit on Sustainable Development in Johannesburg in 2002 and "Rio+20" of 2012.[6] In Africa, Asia, and Latin America, hundreds of integrated landscape initiatives have developed in which public, civil society, and private stakeholders are collaborating to ensure that they all benefit from their landscapes.[7] The table shows a range of examples of different types of MSP, spanning the range from local to global levels of collaboration.

All of these are MSPs

Name	Who is involved?	When?	Goals
Roundtable for Sustainable Palm Oil (RSPO), worldwide. rspo.org	The seven sectors of the palm oil industry: oil palm producers, processors or traders, consumer goods manufacturers, retailers, banks/investors, and environmental/social NGOs	2004 – ongoing	To transform the palm oil industry in collaboration with the global supply chain, and put it on a sustainable path
Market Access for Cattle Herders, West Kenya. http://tinyurl.com/puvg7xk	SNV Netherlands Development Organisation, local government, local small and medium enterprises (SMEs), micro-finance NGOs	2006 – 2009	Setting up local markets to trade cattle
Heart of Borneo, Indonesia/Malaysia/Brunei http://tinyurl.com/p79ot7s	Governments of Indonesia, Malaysia, Brunei, WWF, NGOs	2007– ongoing	Conserving the biodiversity of the Heart of Borneo for the benefit of the people who rely upon it through a network of protected areas, sustainable management of forests, and other sustainable land uses
Landcare, Australia http://tinyurl.com/no459kc	A movement of farmer organisations, government, and environmental NGOs: over 4,000 local community groups	1989 – ongoing	Combating soil salinity and erosion through sound land management practices and sustainable productivity
Regional Dialogue Forum Airport Frankfurt, Germany http://tinyurl.com/ottj3z7	Airport, regional government, citizen initiatives, environmental groups, mayors of surrounding towns, aviation group representatives, chambers of commerce, churches, and unions	2000 – 2008	After several years of mediation, the Forum's task was to continue and deepen the public discourse over specific future solutions for expansion of the airport
Participatory Budgeting in Recife, Brazil http://tinyurl.com/odbjjbx	Local government, citizen groups, NGOs	2001– ongoing	Create more citizen control over public expenditure
Integrated Seed Sector Development, Africa www.issdseed.org	Government, farmer organisations, SMEs, inter-/national seed companies, donors, NGOs and knowledge institutes	2009 – ongoing	To strengthen different seed systems in a country and support the development of a vibrant, pluralistic, and market-oriented seed sector
System of Rice Intensification, Cambodia http://tinyurl.com/q89tkv6	CEDAC (NGO), a movement of over 200,000 farmers, and Cornell University (CIIFAD); now adopted by the Cambodian government	2000 – 2010	Bring Cambodian farming families to food security by improved rice cultivation techniques
World Economic Forum's New Vision for Agriculture: Grow Africa and Grow Asia http://tinyurl.com/pzp9q3n	Alliance between agrifood businesses, government, and civil society to create a more sustainable and inclusive food system	2008 – ongoing	Transforming the agriculture sector by simultaneously delivering food security, environmental sustainability, and economic opportunity
Textile Exchange textileexchange.org	Farmers, manufacturers, brands, and retailers working with organic cotton and sustainable textile production and sales	2002 – ongoing	Accelerating sustainable practices in the textile value chain in order to create material change, restore the environment, and enhance lives around the world.

Characteristics of an MSP

When we talk about multi-stakeholder partnerships, we don't mean 'one-off' workshops or simple multi-actor gatherings. We mean a semi-structured process that helps people to work together on a common problem over a shorter or longer time. But different individuals and groups will relate and engage with each other in different ways.

In practice, MSPs will be very diverse. But a well-functioning MSP is likely to have all or most of the following characteristics:.

Shared and defined 'problem situation' or opportunity: The stakeholders need to share a tangible concern or focus that brings them together. All groups will need to have some sense of why it is worthwhile for them to invest time and energy in the MSP. However, although stakeholders need a common concern in order to start an MSP, the real nature and focus of their concerns and what the group sees as the real problems and opportunities will only fully emerge during the process of developing the MSP.

All the key stakeholders are engaged in the partnership: One of the key features of effective MSPs is that all those who have an influence on or are affected by the situation that sparked the process are involved from the start. Leaving out key groups or involving them too late can quickly undermine an MSP. But as the MSP evolves, the focus may change, meaning that new groups may need to be included and others may drop out. An effective MSP is gender aware, it ensures the voices of women and men, the young and the older are all being heard.

Works across different sectors and scales: For most MSPs, the underlying causes of problems and the opportunities for solutions will be found across different disciplines; across the workings of business, government, and civil society; and across different scales from local to national, and even global.

An MSP is defined more formally by CDI as

"A process of interactive learning, empowerment and participatory governance that enables stakeholders with interconnected problems and ambitions, but often differing interests, to be collectively innovative and resilient when faced with the emerging risks, crises and opportunities of a complex and changing environment."

Follows an agreed but dynamic process and timeframe: Stakeholders need to have some understanding of the process that they are being invited to join and how long it is going to take, before they will commit themselves to take part. But the process needs to be flexible and respond to changing needs. The process and timeframe will evolve over the course of the MSP, but at any one point in time, stakeholders need to have full information about the expected process.

Involves stakeholders in establishing their expectations for a good partnership: Partnerships need to develop clear rules about how people will work together – for example, in terms of communication, decision making, leadership, and responsibilities. But these rules will only work if they are developed and agreed on by those involved. Too often in partnerships, the expectations are not discussed and agreed, which can lead to unnecessary misunderstanding and conflict.

Works with power differences and conflicts: Different stakeholder groups will come to a partnership with different levels of power related to their wealth, status, political connections, knowledge, and communication abilities. If those with most power dominate and those with less power feel excluded or overpowered, the partnership is unlikely to be constructive. Likewise, if conflicts are not recognised and are left 'under the table' to fester, they are likely to become a destructive influence on the partnership process.

Fosters stakeholder learning: The human capacity for innovation and creativity comes from our ability to learn. We can look back and analyse why things may have failed or succeeded, and we can imagine how things could be better. To learn, we have to question and challenge our beliefs and assumptions and think of alternatives. Good MSPs provide a supportive environment with interactive learning processes where people can move beyond their own fixed ideas and positions to see things differently and from the perspective of others.

Balances bottom-up and top-down approaches: Perhaps, in an ideal world, everybody would be involved in all decisions all of the time. But this is simply not feasible, and societies have evolved different mechanisms for delegating decision-making. MSPs need to find a balance between working with structures and decisions that come from the top and supporting input from a wide diversity of stakeholders that comes from the bottom.

Makes transformative and institutional change possible: Most of the issues and challenges we face in the world today are deep-seated. They lie in a mismatch between how the world is now and our past ideas, cultural attitudes, dominant technologies, decision-making mechanisms, and legal frameworks. 'Business as usual' will not help, and we need to focus on transformative change to remove underlying institutional blockages.

MSPs for different purposes

PROBLEM FOCUSED
"What can we do together to solve this problem?"

CONFLICT FOCUSED
"Let's finally sit down and create a way forward out of this deadlock"

OPPORTUNITY FOCUSED
"Let's join forces and create more value for all of us"

Different MSPs for different purposes

What is it that drives people to work together? Is it a common problem? Is it a great opportunity or shared ambition? Is it a desire to overcome conflict and violence? Our experience suggests that any MSP will have a mix of problems, opportunities, and conflicts that shape its underlying dynamics. Some MSPs might start off with a group seeing a great opportunity, but overtime problems and conflicts emerge. Other MSPs might start with a deep conflict, but the process gradually helps people see opportunities for going beyond the sources of the conflict. Often conflict emerges when a particular group perceives that another group is either the cause of the problems they are experiencing, or a threat to their future ambitions and goals.

It is tempting to try to focus your MSP on simply finding a solution to a clearly defined problem. But problem-driven processes don't seem to unlock the creativity, inspiration, and innovation we are seeking. We have learned from experience that for MSPs to achieve deeper, transformational change, we need to start with the ambitions of stakeholders – where they would like to be in future – rather than with problems. We can use these ambitions as a starting point to search together for opportunities. Identifying and working through problems does remain a key part of the MSP process, but it is not the only focus. It is also good to keep in mind that human systems are complex, and that solving one problem all too often just creates a new one that needs resolution.

Whether an MSP is framed as a problem, opportunity, or conflict also depends on the language preferred by the stakeholders who initiate the partnership. The public sector and civil society usually frame an issue as a problem or a conflict to be solved, while the private sector often prefers the more optimistic language of opportunities. One of the key tasks for an MSP facilitator is to clarify the definitions and language used by the stakeholders and to find what can be done together, even though stakeholders may not agree on the way the issue is framed.

People often ask us whether MSPs for business are very different from MSPs initiated by civil society or government. In our experience, MSPs have more in common with each other than they have differences, whether a high-level UN negotiating group or a village-level consortium. This guide is based on the idea that the processes needed to support MSPs are basically similar, even though the situations in which they are being applied are different. But we shouldn't forget that MSPs do differ in detail, and the success of your MSP will depend to a great extent on designing a fitting process for your particular situation.

See Section 3, Designing the process

Who is involved in an MSP?

Who is a stakeholder and who is an outsider in an MSP? A stakeholder is someone who can affect, or is affected by, decisions about an issue that concerns him or her. The issue needs to be carefully delineated. If very broad ('climate change impacts all life on planet earth'), you may end up with an impractically long list of stakeholders to take into account. If too narrow ('climate change impacts village X'), you may miss stakeholders who could be very important for finding a solution. It is really important to analyse both the issue and the stakeholders very carefully.

See Section 6, Choosing tools

We have worked with MSPs initiated by governments, UN bodies, the private sector, civil society, and academics. There are no limits to the type of stakeholder who might take part in an MSP. We are not only talking about formal organisations. Depending on the issue, you might consider working with traditional leaders, individual entrepreneurs, ad hoc citizen initiatives, religious leaders, and sometimes even rebel groups. The rule of thumb is always to have the whole system represented in the conversation, and to aim for a high level of diversity.

Usually MSPs start with one or a few initiators who raise awareness about the issue and gather momentum among a wider stakeholder group. We call this the first circle of stakeholders. They often have the most ownership for driving the agenda of the MSP. When an MSP gets going, these stakeholders are usually represented in a secretariat or steering group. This doesn't mean that other stakeholders are less important. The MSP needs a second circle that follows rather than leads both for legitimacy and for creating a certain reach. And remember that passive stakeholders can, over time, turn into active (first circle) stakeholders and vice versa.

One of our core messages is that facilitation ('making things easy') plays an essential role in getting an MSP to function. By this we don't just mean a professional facilitator who runs the whole MSP development, we mean the whole breadth of facilitating roles. The strongest MSPs have a team of people from the participating stakeholder organisations who feel responsible for facilitating whatever needs to be done. An external facilitator can be a wise investment at particular times, but the internal facilitation team is usually at the core of any success.

See Section 5, From design to practice

The theory behind MSPs

MSPs emerge because stakeholders find that they need to collaborate for change to happen. But there are deeper reasons behind the increasing need for them in the present day. These reasons become clear if you look at recent theories about governance, complex adaptive (human) systems, the human mind (cognition), and innovation. The insights from these theories are embedded throughout the guide, and especially in the principles in Section 4. The detailed theoretical foundations are beyond the scope of the guide, but we have summarised some of the main points briefly below. You can find more detailed sources in the resources (Section 8), if you want to know more.

First, governance is changing. The modern world has become globalised. Economic activity and environmental and social issues don't respect national borders, and this challenges the dominance of the nation state. Governments face issues of risk and uncertainty that they cannot address on their own. At the same time, people expect greater democracy, government is becoming more decentralised, and social media are having a huge influence on decision-making. The need for more participatory forms of governance is increasing – which is in line with the approach of MSPs. MSPs can complement the formal structures of government at local, national, or international scales.

Second, human societies are 'complex adaptive systems'. This means that change happens as a result of the combined actions of many individuals who are all interconnected in the system. Nobody is in full control, and change happens in unexpected and surprising ways. This means we must constantly adapt to new and often unforeseen circumstances. One way of improving the adaptability and resilience of such a system is to increase the efficiency of communication, which is exactly what MSPs do. The insights from systems and complexity science give a strong justification to the process of MSPs.

Third, the human mind is astounding. Our cognitive processes are often represented as a simplified form of rational economic thinking and selfishness, but this is not how we operate. Humans are cooperative, creative, and emotional people – and they need to feel valued and respected. The approach to MSPs that we offer in this guide, and the tools we propose to help groups to work together, put into practice much of what we now know about human cognition.

Finally, the science of governance, systems, and cognition together provides a better understanding of innovation and collaboration. Human societies are constantly innovating, coming up with new technologies and new ways of organising and managing themselves. Increasingly sophisticated and rapid forms of innovation will be needed to tackle the big issues that the world faces, such as climate change. And MSPs are an important way of enhancing innovation.

Designing and facilitating an MSP Process

No matter how straightforward it may seem, an effective MSP process doesn't just happen – it needs to be designed.[8] Design is about creating something that works well for its intended function. In the case of an MSP, this means creating processes that help stakeholder engagement to function smoothly. You will need to carefully think through, plan, implement, and review each step in the process. But we don't mean that you simply develop a 'grand plan' at the beginning and keep following it. Rather, at any given moment you, and the MSP group, should think about what the whole process is trying to achieve and decide what would be the most sensible next step. The approach is described in detail in Section 3.

So what does the process of an MSP look like in practice? An important part of building effective partnerships is bringing the different stakeholders together in workshops, meetings, and dialogue. Bilateral meetings between groups and individual meetings of stakeholder groups may also be useful. Other activities will range from gaining the support of leaders and influential figures, to capacity building of stakeholders, background research, logistical coordination, and communications and media support. The whole process is 'oiled' by facilitation. This means individuals and groups accepting responsibility for acting as convenors, moderators, and catalysts in the process. We discuss this in more detail in Section 5.

When is an MSP the right choice?

Developing an MSP can be a long, time-consuming, and expensive process. And participating in an MSP may tie up limited resources that are needed elsewhere. You need to think carefully before deciding that an MSP is the best way to approach your particular concern. Is an MSP the only way to address your issue? Is it the most cost-effective way? Will it lead to additional benefits that will be important for other activities? Will the reward be sufficient? Or could there be better, faster, or more efficient ways to achieve the same result? What might your constituency think when you join such an initiative? Will your organisation be co-opted? Might your company suffer damage to its

A decision helper: pros and cons of MSPs	Advantages...	Limits....
	• Can address a more complex issue than you can tackle alone	• Requires time and resources to design and implement properly
	• Partners can access complementary skills and resources from each other	• Can only work if there is sufficient representation from stakeholders
	• Results will have broader ownership (more sustainable)	• Will often not deliver short-term success: patience is required
	• Learning and collaboration increases chance of systemic change	• Not easy to find funding for processes that are relatively open-ended and the topics of which may evolve over time
		• Success is never guaranteed

reputation? How do you know which collaboration is likely to pay off? Think carefully about why you think change will happen through collaboration. One way of doing this is by expressing your 'Theory of Change'. This means answering the question: 'How do we think change will happen?' Making this explicit, with all the assumptions that are often made unconsciously, can help you decide whether an MSP is really a suitable option.

See Chapter 3, Phase 2: Adaptive planning

As a rule of thumb, MSPs are not useful when a problem or opportunity can be tackled by a single person or organisation. They are only useful when a challenge is complex, and the results will depend on the actions and linkages between the different actors.

See Section 4, Principle 1: Embrace systemic change

The timing is also important. Maybe initiatives have already been started on similar issues with the same stakeholder groups, in which case you may find it better to align with these existing structures if you have access. Maybe it is too early for an MSP: you need to do more groundwork to convince others it is worth their effort, or there is still too much volatility and lack of trust for collaboration to be possible. This means you should start by raising awareness and building trust before developing the MSP. Maybe the resources are simply not available at the present time, and you need to do more work to secure funding. In this case, you might focus on more limited elements that your organisation can address alone, and plan for an MSP at a later date.

There will be many situations where investing in an MSP will be the only way to achieve real success, and you will need to convince everyone concerned that the long-term benefit will more than justify the investment. But if there is a simpler way to address your problem effectively, then don't engage in an MSP.

The business case for MSPs

How an investment in community engagement by an Indonesian palm oil company generated a large return on investment. If you think that engaging your stakeholders is too costly, think again. A palm oil company suffered protests and roadblocks at their first plantation that cost an estimated $ 15 million in lost revenue. They calculated that early engagement with communities could generate a Return on Investment (ROI) of 880% for each day of disruption they could avoid. A typical 10,000-hectare plantation has a mill that processes up to 60 tonnes of fresh palm fruit bunches per hour. In the peak season, the mill runs for 22 hours per day, 6 days a week, which makes it difficult to catch up any lost days. With fruit bunches selling for $ 200 per tonne, the cost of a day of disruption would be $ 264,000. A community engagement programme costing $ 30,000 would show a return on investment (ROI) of 880% if it helped avoid a single day of disruption. The company didn't only profit by avoiding lost revenue; it found that early engagement with the community offered many more benefits. It helped to build trust with the community and also to identify existing land ownership structures before land brokers had a chance to get involved, which can complicate matters for both the community and the company.

Source: WWF (2012),[9] *Courtesy of Earth Security Initiative/CDC Group.*

3 DESIGNING THE PROCESS
The key elements for developing an MSP

This section introduces a process model that you can use for designing and developing your MSP. The model outlines the main phases of an MSP and the key considerations for effective stakeholder collaboration. The model operates like a GPS: it will help you (and your partners) identify your position and the direction to take in the journey you are making with stakeholders. The success of your MSP will depend largely on your ability to design a suitable process that includes conceptualisation, planning, and continuous adjustment and redesign.

UNDERSTANDING
THE CONTEXT

USING
PARTICIPATORY
METHODS AND
TOOLS

An evolving and
adaptive
multi-stakeholder
partnership
process

DEVELOPING
CHANGE
STRATEGIES

Process matters

No matter how straightforward it may seem, an effective MSP process doesn't just happen – it needs to be designed. By design we mean consciously thinking through and planning the activities and events that are needed to achieve your desired outcomes and what is likely to work best at the particular stage and with the particular dynamics of your MSP (see box for examples of typical activities). Remember, a good design in any field is something that works well for the needs of its users in a given context. There will never be a simple recipe or blueprint; rather, you will need to follow an iterative process together with the stakeholders in which you assess the present situation, plan, implement, review, adjust, and again plan ahead. As leading social entrepreneur Liam Black[1] points out: "Be strong on your mission but flexible on the details of how you get there". Sometimes you may seem to take two steps forward and one back, often it will be necessary to experiment to find out what works. The key is to continually respond to the changing situation.

There are three main areas to think about in the design
1) Understanding the context.
2) Developing a change strategy guided by the MSP principles and process model.
3) Deciding on the methodologies and tools that will be used to engage stakeholders in relationship building, analysis, planning, and collective action.

Designing the activities and organising events can seem quite daunting, not least because you are likely to be facing a wide range of strategic, relational, and logistical issues, all demanding your attention. The priorities will also change over time as the MSP evolves. In this section, we outline a process model that you can use to guide you through the different steps. It will help you to locate yourself in a particular phase, and to identify and address critical questions in each phase – rather like having a GPS for process design.

Types of MSP activities and events: options for design

• Preparation and planning meetings involving those who are initiating, organising, or facilitating the MSP
• Individual or small group meetings with key people whose support and influence are critical
• Meetings of a steering or advisory group established to help guide and support the overall MSP process
• Multi-stakeholder workshops involving various combinations of relevant stakeholders
• Single-stakeholder workshops that enable a single group or sector to prepare for engaging in the MSP
• Working groups that undertake specific organisational, research or communication activities
• Field visits and study tours
• Seminars or conferences that engage a wider audience
• Media events

The process model

Every MSP process is unique and will follow its own path and logic, but there are common phases and process considerations. Essentially, the process model captures these in outline to give you a structure for planning and a checklist[2] to make sure you haven't overlooked anything. The four main phases are iterative; you will continually revisit them as your MSP progresses.

1. Initiating
- Clarify reasons for an MSP
- Undertake initial situation analysis (stakeholders, issues, institutions, power and politics)
- Establish interim steering body
- Build stakeholder support
- Establish scope and mandate
- Outline the process

2. Adaptive planning
- Deepen understanding and trust
- Identify issues and opportunities
- Generate visions for the future
- Examine future scenarios
- Agree on strategies for change
- Identify actions and responsibilities
- Communicate outcomes

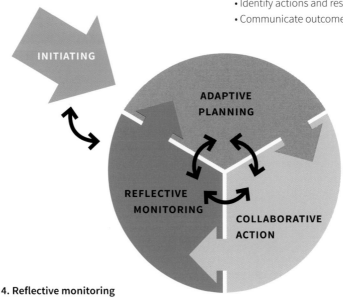

4. Reflective monitoring
- Create a learning culture and environment
- Define success criteria and indicators
- Develop and implement monitoring mechanisms
- Review progress and generate lessons
- Use lessons for improvement

3. Collaborative action
- Develop detailed action plans
- Secure resources and support
- Develop capacities for action
- Establish management structures
- Manage implementation
- Maintain stakeholder commitment

Phase 1: Initiating

MSPs start in many different ways. It can be through the inspiration of a single individual, the frustration of a conflict, as part of a government policy process, or even through an accidental 'meeting of minds'. No matter the origin, you (and those working with you) should consider the following questions during the start-up phase.

Are the reasons for starting the MSP clear? You need to be sure that the planned MSP is a viable option. Stakeholders will only be interested in and motivated to engage in the MSP if they understand why it would be useful and how it would benefit their interests. Over time, the reasons for the MSP may evolve and change, but at the start, there needs to be enough clarity to spark engagement.

Have the overall dynamics of the situation been adequately explored? When you are working to get an MSP off the ground, it is essential to first understand the context. Who are the important stakeholders and what are their interests and ambitions? Who are the key leaders? What are the politics of the situation and are there overt or underlying conflicts? Who has the power to help drive or undermine the initiative? You need to know the answers to these questions in order to frame the MSP in a way that will enable initial buy-in from the stakeholders. Later, your understanding of the context will need to be deepened with all stakeholders as the process unfolds.

See Section 6, Tools 5, 10, 11 and 12: Stake- holder Analysis

Have respected champions been mobilised? First impressions are important! The stakeholders' view of those initiating, organising, and/or supporting the MSP can fundamentally influence what unfolds and long-term success. The people taking a lead must be seen as legitimate and be respected for being open and fair, even if they are aligned with a particular stakeholder group. It can be very important to have respected leaders from all the different stakeholder groups showing their support for the initiative. As soon as one stakeholder group perceives the process as being hijacked by another group, legitimacy will collapse.

Is there a legitimate steering group in place? In general, a group representing different interests will take responsibility for getting the process going. The way in which different stakeholder groups view the initiative will be strongly influenced by who is involved with and who is leading this group, so great care

"At first, our Uganda AgriHub organised two-day networking events in the capital, which were great for exchange and learning. But the private sector did not show up until we tried something different: full-day events with a networking cocktail late afternoon. Businesses turned up, as they considered it an efficient way to pick up the knowledge of the day and develop business contacts. And once we started organising agri-business fairs in rural areas, the private sector even started sponsoring our events. In short, find their interest – which is doing business – and they come." - Roel Snelder AgriProFocus

is needed. In some cases, an independent facilitator or organisation may take on the mobilising role, in which case they must be seen as a legitimate and neutral player open to all groups.

Has stakeholder support been established? As a golden rule, the earlier people are consulted, listened to, and given a chance to contribute, the more likely they are to be supportive. You can help build stakeholder support in the early stages by holding informal bilateral discussions. You should also inform people generally about what is happening in ways that speak to their issues and interests. Involving one or two representatives from a stakeholder group can backfire if there is no feedback to the rest of the group. Pay attention in the early stages to ensuring that stakeholders develop a feeling of trust in the process.

Are the mandate and scope of the MSP clear? Under what auspices or authority is the MSP being established? Is it linked to a formal government process? Is it a voluntary process by the stakeholders? Is there any legal backing? It is really important to have a clear definition of the mandate, authority, and decision-making powers of the MSP, and to communicate this clearly to all concerned. You should also be as clear as possible about the scope of the issues the MSP plans to deal with. Inevitably, this will evolve over time. However, at the start stakeholders need to have some understanding of how broad or narrow the agenda will be.

Is there an outline of the process? What is expected from the different stakeholders? What meetings and activities will be held and when? What sort of time commitment will be required, by whom? Stakeholders will want to know in general, but practical, terms what the process will mean for them. They will also be interested in how final decisions will be made, and by whom.

Challenges in the Initiating Phase	How to address these?	
Whom to invite, whom to leave out?	Carry out an initial stakeholder mapping to make sure the 'must-haves' are on your list. Aim for 3–8 committed stakeholders from different sectors; remember that the core group should be agile and not too large at this stage.	See Section 6, Tools 5, 10, 11 and 12
Analysis or action first?	Researchers will plea for more analysis upfront, activists may want action to start straightaway. It is not an either/or decision. Early actions can create engagement and trust. Good analysis is critical but in complex systems the insights often come from testing things out. Propose action research and balance the thinking and the doing.	
What is the common concern?	Don't rush! People will need time to understand the common concerns and find shared goals. Be careful of setting strategies and action plans before it is clear what you really want to achieve. Try to agree on an overarching common goal, but there is no need as yet to define the strategies on how to get there. You can also agree to disagree on the strategies. Make this explicit in your Partnership Agreement.	
What if a key stakeholder has no interest?	Respect their view, but try to find out under what conditions they might consider joining. Ask permission to contact the stakeholder again in say six months to give them an update.	See Section 5: Getting Organised

Phase 2: Adaptive planning

See Section 4,
Principle 1:
Embrace sys-
temic change

Adaptive planning means developing plans based on the present situation, and adjusting them as the situation changes. Essentially it is 'responsive' rather than 'prescriptive'. You can read more about the concept in the next section. Planning for your MSP involves engaging stakeholders to work out what change is needed, and exploring how to bring that change about. This is not always easy, as stakeholders may disagree on both what and how. The adaptive approach avoids cumbersome discussions about 'the plan to be agreed on' and uses the planning process itself to help participants agree step-by-step on what is needed. Instead of a detailed master plan, you can develop a roadmap with stakeholders that shows the end goal and proposes several complementary pathways that can help the MSP move towards that goal. Detailed choices on which pathway to use will be made later based on feedback and testing. In other words, you are building a joint Theory of Change with stakeholders as you go along (see box). Stakeholders will have different theories of change on the issue, and you will need to help the group develop a joint perspective. Be explicit about the assumptions you are making, as this will help you to ask the right questions when you review or test your theory of change. It is important to ensure that diverse stakeholders are involved at this stage representing multiple perspectives and ideas.

Once the broad approach and major steps are clear, you will want to focus on more detailed planning. This may involve just a few people, rather than the whole group. For example, stakeholders may decide that it would be good to have a two-day interaction in the early stages for everyone to meet. The meeting facilitator (or a small group) will select the best tools and activities to build trust and understanding between these particular stakeholders, and then work with the organiser on the details of the arrangements. Remember that even little details – for example, how people are welcomed and how chairs are arranged – can have a large impact on the longer-term success of the MSP.

What is Theory of Change?

We refer to Theory of Change as the understanding of how change happens. By articulating your ToC you can clarify how your MSP initiative can contribute to the desired change. Typically, a ToC is quite honest about assumptions that are made in the strategies chosen. Many organisations use ToC thinking as a requirement for initiatives that aim to address a complex challenge. See www.theoryofchange.nl

You should consider the following questions during this phase:

Are understanding and trust being developed between stakeholders?
Before any decisions can be made or action taken around difficult issues,
stakeholders need to understand each others' views, values, perspectives,
and interests. They don't need to agree, but people need to feel understood,
listened to, and respected before they will be willing to cooperate. Take time
to build trust between people in the early stages of adaptive planning and
don't move too quickly to making decisions. Start with activities that help
people to get to know each other. Humour and fun can be the best enablers!

See Section 6,
Tool 41:
Visioning

Have visions for the future been generated? When people disagree, it can be
helpful to move to a higher level where there is a wider basis for agreement.
Different stakeholder groups often share deeper values and interests in the
bigger picture. Developing visions for the future is a good way of finding
shared ambitions. Collaboration driven by a positive vision of the future is
also more inspiring than simply solving immediate problems and complaints.
You don't need to generate a single shared vision, multiple visions of the
future will help you to explore commonality and identify the potential for
working together on shared ambitions and interests.

**Have the issues and opportunities for different stakeholder groups been
identified?** You need to have a good understanding of all the different issues
(problems) and opportunities that different stakeholder groups see or
experience. You also need to remember that stakeholder groups will identify
different issues and opportunities within the group. Mapping the different
perceived issues and opportunities will help stakeholders gain a much better
understanding of the overall situation, and where there is commonality and
where differences.

See Section 6,
Tool 36:
Scenario
Planning

Have different scenarios been examined? Quite often, people will not have
thought very far into the future about the consequences of current trends
and behaviours. And in a complex world, the future is impossible to predict.
Scenario thinking is a good way of helping stakeholders to ask the question,
"what would happen if…". The idea is to consider a range of different
possible futures. These are developed around 'critical uncertainties': areas
where change is likely, but the nature of the change is hard to predict. For
example, what are the different scenarios for a business if coffee commodity
prices stay the same or become much higher? What would be the impact
on agriculture of different levels of climate change? Looking at different
scenarios is a great way to help stakeholders think outside the box and
examine their often-unquestioned assumptions about the future. Engaging
in the process can open people's eyes to new perspectives and the concerns of
other stakeholders.

Have strategies for change been agreed upon? Ultimately, decisions will have to be made based on the best available understanding and analysis about what to do and what strategy to follow – otherwise nothing will change. This is where MSPs can become most difficult. You need to be careful about the timing. Too early, without enough trust building or collective analysis, and it will be difficult to reach agreement. Too late, and stakeholders may become disillusioned with the process and withdraw. You don't need to aim for a 'grand plan'. Your strategy could be a set of principles to follow, actions for different stakeholders to follow up on individually, or a series of experiments or pilots to test options. Develop a clear plan for monitoring and for revisiting the strategy so that it can be adapted as necessary.

Have responsibilities been agreed upon? To put a strategy into practice, it must be clear who will take responsibility for what and whether they have the capacity and resources to do so.

Are the outcomes of the process being shared and well communicated? It is impossible for everyone to be involved in all aspects of an MSP. Much of the detailed adaptive planning work will probably be done by a smaller representative group. You will need to make sure that the outcomes and decisions of the planning process are constantly communicated and explained to the wider stakeholder and constituency groups. If this fails, you may lose support, as the wider community may not understand why particular decisions have been taken.

See Section 5, Getting Organised

Challenges in the Adaptive Planning Phase	How to address these?
Can latecomers still join?	The more the merrier - but can you manage it? Distinguish between a core group (or steering committee or carrying group) and a second ring of participants who can join but will not be involved in oversight or major decisions. Perform the 'Influence/Importance Matrix' exercise in Section 6 to map which stakeholders you must have on board. Prioritise the essential ones, but also look out for underrepresented stakeholders.
Going deeper, or going faster?	You will notice different preferences of stakeholders for pacing the MSP. Balancing these preferences is an art, not a science. Remember that not everybody needs to do all things together, all of the time. See Section 4 for tips on this issue.
Agreeing on the MSP strategy	Accept that it will be impossible to have all stakeholders agree on all aspects of what the MSP should do. Invest in developing a shared Theory of Change that can become a strong unifying factor for the MSP.

See Section 6, Tool 12

See Section 4, Perspective 3: Balancing results and relationships

Phase 3: Collaborative action

See Section 4, Principle 6: Collaborative leadership

It is one thing to strategise and plan, it is quite another to put the ideas into action. Not all MSPs go to the action phase. Some simply provide the agreements, directions, and policies for others to follow. But some MSPs do need to follow through on action. One of the criticisms of MSPs is that too often they don't put ideas into practice. This is understandable as a very different level of organisation, management, and resourcing is needed to move into a phase of collaborative action. Stakeholders may also find the adaptive planning phase more exciting and interesting, and lose enthusiasm when the hard work comes along. Thinking through the collaborative action phase can make all the difference to the success of your MSP.

You should consider the following questions:

Have action plans been developed? Even in a highly adaptive planning process, where the overall strategy is constantly being improved, plans are needed for who is going to do what, when, and how. This is especially important in an MSP where there are many different players. Sometimes stakeholders may only realise there are problems with the overall strategy when they get down to detailed action planning. You will need an iterative process between improving and updating the overall strategy and carrying out detailed planning.

Have resources and support been secured? You will generally need resources (money, time, equipment, expertise) to implement the agreed strategy. The stakeholder groups may need to commit resources, or there may be an opportunity to obtain funding from third parties. Moving from the adaptive planning to the collaborative action phase will often mean you need to mobilise support.

See Section 4, Belbin Team Roles; and Section 6, Tool 35

Do stakeholders have the capacity needed to take action? Make sure that you draw capable people from diverse stakeholders and arrange teams that complement each other well. Of course, there will be gaps. At the same time, an MSP can be a great way to develop skills and capacities. In fact, we have found that the opportunity to obtain new knowledge, skills, and networks can be a key incentive for stakeholders to remain active in an MSP. This is especially true if the MSP uses participatory learning tools as part of its core activity.

Are the necessary organisational structures in place? The MSP may require a more solid management structure at this stage, especially if it has been successful in mobilising resources. The management structure could be a coordination unit (hosted by a lead partner), an independent secretariat, or a backbone organisation. However, strong management structures always carry the risk that they overshadow or even compete with the other partners in the MSP, so open alliances are becoming more common. These decentralised network arrangements are designed to drive innovation through an open-ended framework, unlike an invitation-only alliance.[3] It is also important at

See Section 5, Getting Organised

this stage to revisit the governance structure of the MSP. Which body makes the decisions? Who are the patrons and what is their role? What legal form is appropriate?

Is stakeholder commitment being maintained? Initiators of MSPs often move on. And new people come on board who may or may not have the skills to deal with the challenges of the specific phase of the MSP. This turnover is a risk, as much tacit knowledge about the MSP can disappear. The MSP core team should check regularly that participants are satisfied with their roles, sufficiently challenged, and have enough support to do their part. Include the question "Are you still happy with the role you are playing in this team?" in your annual progress review. Remember, too, that distant stakeholders also need to be kept informed in order to maintain or (re)build commitment. Make sure that plans and results are communicated to stakeholders on the fringes.

Challenges in the Collaborative Action Phase	How to address these?
Keeping motivation up when things move slow.	This is the phase where the MSP usually suffers from setbacks, as reality is stubborn. It might be necessary to review your overall goal and perhaps make it less ambitious. Another tactic is to identify intermediate goals and celebrate them actively when they are achieved.
How to avoid over-formalizing an MSP	The best MSPs remain adaptive and agile in this mature phase. This is a challenge because of the natural tendency to formalise and structure as much as we can (especially in the public sector). Our advice is to look carefully at the content of the partnership agreement: the emphasis should be on principles in the partnership, not only on technical details of roles and responsibilities.
Keeping commitment from participating organisations	An organisation that decided to join an MSP may allocate some budget and staff time to it - but this does not mean that decision makers are fully aware of how the MSP is progressing. Try to create packages of information that the MSP champions can take back to their organisations so they can continue to sell the MSP to their colleagues.
Over reliance on a facilitator or broker	In this guide, we suggest that you involve qualified facilitators or partnership brokers in MSPs. But if they end up dominating, there is something wrong. Any facilitator should consider their intervention as time-bound, and should build new capacities among MSP participants to transfer responsibilities as soon as can be done responsibly.

Phase 4: Reflective monitoring

See Section 4, Principle 1: Embrace systemic change and Section 4, Principle 7: Foster participatory learning

The Reflective Monitoring phase lies at the centre of the MSP process model, embedded in the other phases. In other words, reflective monitoring is something you should do continuously in all phases. People tend to think of monitoring as something to do when it's time to prepare a report, often at the very end of the project. But monitoring can be one of your most valuable resources – the best way to learn about what is working and what isn't, and what you should change. Reflective monitoring is an integral part of adaptive management and is critical for building learning loops into activities. As well as the more formal monitoring – which involves research and data gathering – regular reflection moments will help participants to think about what they are doing (outcomes/result), how they are doing it (process), and how the lessons learned can be used to improve future work. These moments can also be used to reflect on the results of more formal monitoring activities. Reflection will make the planning more robust and the actions more innovative and focused. You should integrate reflection moments into your process from the earliest phase, preferably as a regular habit (weekly, monthly, half-yearly). We usually organise these reflection moments as a part of existing rhythms. For example, rather than organising a specific reflection workshop, use a few hours of the yearly planning workshop to critically reflect.

See Section 6, Tool 56

Monitoring is also a product

Performance measurement can be an important product of an MSP. Take the Extractives Industry Transparency Initiative (EITI), an action network of governments, civil society, and business to increase transparency in the extractives industry.[4] For EITI, measuring the progress of companies towards an established goal in an objective and verifiable way is key to the initiative, and specific metrics are defined and collected. By building performance measurement tools, the MSP can make an important contribution to the field, and represents value addition. It helps set standards and shows who is doing well and who is lagging behind, and is thus another piece in the puzzle in the move towards a more sustainable industry.

Use the following questions to guide the reflective monitoring:

See Section 6,
Tool 56:
Reflection

Has a learning culture and environment been created? This means reflecting regularly on successes and failures in order to adapt the vision and actions to the situation. Typical reflection questions could include: What happened? Why? So what? Now what? Use the following guidelines to help create a learning culture: 1) Make participants feel that their ideas and suggestions are valued; 2) Consider mistakes and failures as important for learning, and not as embarrassing; 3) Ensure that implementers, including primary stakeholders, regularly and informally discuss progress, relationships, and improvements; 4) Lead by example: listen carefully to others and consciously seek solutions together; and 5) Set aside time for discussing mistakes and learning lessons during regular meetings and workshops.

Have success criteria been defined? The stakeholders should first agree on what they need to know in order to take decisions. Then you can define performance or evaluation questions that focus on these key information needs. For example, 'To what extent has our MSP influenced policy makers? Why (not)?' Finally, you need to define indicators that will help you to answer the key questions. For example 'Types of changes initiated by policy makers who attended advocacy meetings'.

Have monitoring mechanisms been developed and implemented? In order to establish a monitoring mechanism, the MSP will need to develop a shared strategy and action plan for data collection and processing; analysis, critical reflection, and decision making; communication and reporting; capacities and conditions; incentives for monitoring and evaluation (M&E); a management information system; and financial resources.

More information on how to develop monitoring systems can be found at www.managingforimpact.org

Has progress been reviewed and evaluated and lessons identified? MSPs should be reviewed and evaluated like projects, although the methodologies might differ. You are still looking for answers to the key evaluation questions of impact, relevance, sustainability, effectiveness, and efficiency. Make sure that you have a good balance of content indicators and process indicators. Document the lessons learned according to the following format:

· Theme of 'lessons learned'
· What was our original understanding or assumption?
· What is our revised understanding or assumption?
· One or two examples that substantiate the new understanding
· How did the project/process come to this insight?

Have the lessons learned been fed back into the strategy and implementation procedures? The lessons learned should lead to changes being made in the various aspects of your initiative, including process, structure, management, reporting, and communicating. Is the story being told of how you have adapted or are encouraging people to adapt? Has learning been fed back into the practices you are currently undertaking or planning for the future? Are you using the lessons learned to fine tune both the initiative/project, and the actual process of monitoring and evaluation?

Challenges in the Reflective Monitoring Phase	How to address these?
Doing reflection activities with busy leaders and executives	Reflection and learning are often regarded as 'nice to haves', rather than core business. Rather than calling it 'reflection' or 'learning', we often use words like 'strategy review' or 'performance enhancement' or 'looking back and looking forward'. In these conversations, we can address the same questions (What happened? Why? So what? Now what?).
Who should do the monitoring?	Ideally, everybody is involved. But in reality, this role will be played by specific people in the secretariat or backbone organisation. Tip: make sure to develop management summaries of progress data so that the monitoring outcomes are discussed by the leadership, and make visuals (e.g., infographics) to communicate progress to the outside world.
Who should do the evaluation?	Learning involves creating meaning. What matters most in an MSP is the meaning that stakeholders attach to what is being achieved, rather than expert judgement or external evaluation. There is still a place for external support – for example, if results are disputed or if a donor requires it. Make sure you have a qualified evaluation team using methods that help the stakeholders utilise the learning.
People don't open up and admit what really happened	This displays a lack of trust. Reflection and learning can be important relationship building opportunities between organisations. But be careful: it is not acceptable to look in someone else's kitchen and criticise the food. The first task is to work on mutual trust in the team. Consider using appreciative inquiry (AI) to emphasise the positive aspects of the MSP.

See Section 6, Tool 6: Appreciative Story Telling

Process design in practice

MSPs can take many forms. The forms will differ from situation to situation, and may even change over time. Nevertheless, activities usually follow a similar sequence, as shown in the timeline of activities in a hypothetical MSP. In reality, timelines can vary from half a year to several years.

Over the lifespan of such an MSP process, many decisions need to be made: some by a core group of initiators and facilitators, and some by all stakeholders involved. Section 5 introduces practical aspects, which can help a facilitation team to lead an MSP effectively throughout all four phases.

A good MSP is clearly 'more than just meetings',[5] but good meetings and workshops are essential to make progress and are a major component in the practice of process design. Holding good meetings is something of an art, but as a first step, you need to be clear about the purpose. The overall purpose of MSP meetings may shift over time from influencing, to innovating, developing foresight, and aligning and acting. But in all cases, they will provide learning and networking opportunities. The following flowchart from GATHER[6] will help you to express the primary purpose of your MSP event. Once you have the purpose clear, you will be able to choose the appropriate process designs and tools for the meeting.

See Section 6:
Tools

Defing the purpose of your MSP meeting

First cover the fundamentals

Then choose a primary purpose

Engage a diverse range of stakeholders, reflecting different facets of the problem. Help them connect with one another, build trusting relationships, and discover shared areas of commonality

BUILD NETWORKS

SHARE LEARNING

Enable participants to exchange information, expertise, and points of view in a form that benefits their individual and collective practices.

Influence

Shape the attitudes of key stakeholders and public by inviting leaders and decision makers to discuss your initial proposals; use their perspectives to sharpen the ideas and then use the resulting product to promote broader conversations and action.

Innovate

Explore new approaches and enable creative disruption by reframing, reimagining, or recombining different elements and perspectives. Use these inputs to prototype transformational new processes or services and to develop ideas for their adoption and scaling.

Develop foresight

Anticipate potential challenges and identify new opportunities for intervention by collecting information on how the world is evolving today and diverse perpectives about the directions that it could take in the future.

Align & act

Mobilise stakeholders in different parts of the system to act in a coordinated way. Help build a shared understanding of het system and the problem, develop consensus around a common vision, align strategies around it, and support one another in execution.

You should prepare a clear agenda and proposed timeline for the meeting to guide stakeholder expectations, help participants to prepare, and help ensure that all the proposed topics are discussed. We give two generic outlines on the next pages to illustrate the possible flow and elements of a meeting agenda. They are taken from typical meetings facilitated by CDI: one half-day meeting and one three-day workshop. These are not blueprints; they are provided to illustrate the logic behind meetings and some possible combinations. In practice, we actually end up fine-tuning and changing the design as we go along in almost all meetings, in response to the group dynamics and particular needs.

Timeline of a hypothetical MSP over the course of a year

Time frame in months

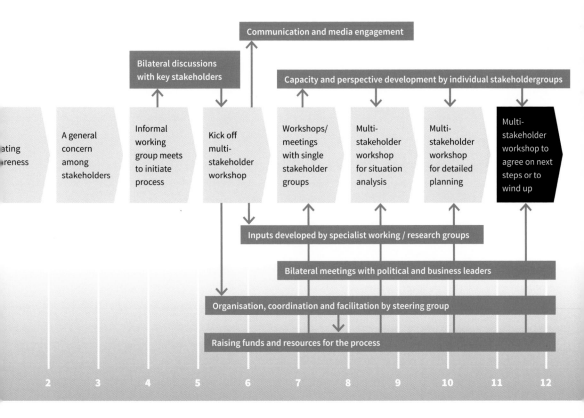

Example of a 3-day stakeholder meeting

Purpose: to align different stakeholders in a new partnership, deepen participants' understanding of the issue at hand, and co-create an agenda for future action. There are 30 participants from 8 countries.

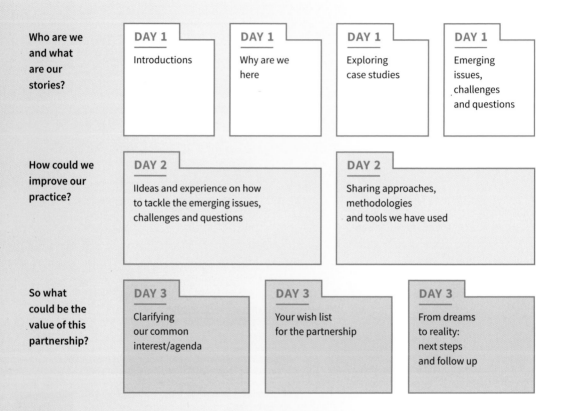

Who are we and what are our stories?

DAY 1
Introductions

DAY 1
Why are we here

DAY 1
Exploring case studies

DAY 1
Emerging issues, challenges and questions

How could we improve our practice?

DAY 2
IIdeas and experience on how to tackle the emerging issues, challenges and questions

DAY 2
Sharing approaches, methodologies and tools we have used

So what could be the value of this partnership?

DAY 3
Clarifying our common interest/agenda

DAY 3
Your wish list for the partnership

DAY 3
From dreams to reality: next steps and follow up

Notes

- This meeting had a very open, explorative nature. Participants were carefully selected based on their track records on the issue (sustainable agriculture) in different sectors. We shared in advance who was coming, and asked participants to bring cases that could inspire other participants.
- Much time was taken for participants to get to know each other and discuss their motives for change making rather than their formal positions. Hence the question 'Why are we here?' This set the tone for participants to connect on a deeper level than just talking about possible activities or 'who fits where in this partnership'.
- The outcomes of the meeting were not predefined. Yet, it was important to document, summarise, and double-check the ideas and agreements that emerged during the meeting. This process tracing is essential in explorative dialogue meetings.
- During the meeting, ideas that emerged were translated into tasks that small groups could work on. This task orientation helped people to align more easily and deliver tangible outcomes.

Example of a half-day stakeholder meeting

Purpose: Influencing by obtaining quality stakeholder feedback on an issue paper. Engage stakeholders for future collaboration. 40–60 participants, one afternoon session

Notes

- This meeting has no spectacular participatory methodology. You will find that, in formal settings, people can be unwilling to move away from traditional ways of convening, or it may be inappropriate. Still you can tweak the design to include short break-out sessions and buzz sessions with two or three participants to increase participation and sharing of perspectives.
- Be clear that you cannot use such a short meeting to agree on a common goal unless the group has already done a lot of groundwork prior to the meeting. In this case, the aim was to obtain quality feedback on an idea, and hopefully increased buy-in from a range of stakeholders.
- Chatham House Rule[7] At a meeting held under the Chatham House Rule, anyone who comes to the meeting is free to use information from the discussion, but is not allowed to reveal who made any comment. The rule is designed to increase the openness of discussions.
- Be very clear how you will document the feedback, and arrange rapporteurs and formats. Agree beforehand how you will share back to participants.

14:00
Welcome and introductions (agenda overview, Chatham House Rule)

14:20
Overview of the issue and the initiative (intro by coordinator)

14:40
Discussion on issue paper (mixed small groups)

15:20
Challenges and opportunities (plenary inventory of key points)

16:40
Harvesting feedback (buzz groups of 3-5 people, paper format provided)

17:20
Wrap up, next steps (plenary summary by chair)

Questions for designing an MSP process

- Think about a meeting, conference, or workshop that you've attended that went really well. What was it about the design – either prior to or at the event itself – that contributed to its effectiveness?
- Consider an upcoming meeting that you are planning in your MSP. Using the elements of the Process Model that we have explored in this section, what elements might you pay more attention to in your planning to help set a conversational tone and invite a greater diversity of perspectives towards the outcomes that you're seeking?
- Imagine that your MSP has no budget for organising meetings or workshops. What could you still do to move towards your goals – without meetings?
- What are some mistakes or missed opportunities in your MSP? How could you maximise learning from these mistakes?

4 SEVEN PRINCIPLES THAT MAKE MSPS EFFECTIVE

We have formulated seven principles that will help you to make your MSP more effective. The principles are based on our experience as well as on interaction with academics and practitioners. Each principle has a theoretical underpinning and descriptions of practical application. For each principle, there are three or four perspectives – these are conceptual models and theoretical ideas that help to explain the principle and illustrate the practical implications.

The first principle is perhaps the most challenging to understand. But don't be put off: the ideas of complexity and complex adaptive systems are important for understanding how groups respond to change, and the extent to which you can and can't predict outcomes and plan for success. The basic concepts are introduced, but for a deeper understanding, there are many other resources available to draw on in this rapidly developing interdisciplinary field.

PRINCIPLE 1

Embrace systemic change

1. Assessing the complexity of a situation
2. Soft systems methodology
3. Adaptive management
4. Four quadrants of change

PRINCIPLE 2

Transform institutions

1. Supporting and obstructing institutions
2. Systems thinking
3. Framework for institutional analysis
4. Linking institutional change

PRINCIPLE 3

Work with power

1. Types of power
2. Rank
3. Expressions of power
4. Faces of power
5. Empowerment

PRINCIPLE 4

Deal with conflict

1. Causes of conflict
2. Continuum of conflict
3. Interest based negotiation

PRINCIPLE 5

Communicate effectively

1. Dialogue
2. Non-violent communication
3. Powerful questions and active listening
4. Cultural issues and communication

PRINCIPLE 6

Promote collaborative leadership

1. Six aspects of leadership
2. Belbin Team Roles
3. Balancing results and relationships

PRINCIPLE 7

Foster participatory learning

1. Experiential learning cycle
2. Learning styles
3. Single, double, triple loop learning

Simon Zadek*

"Partners think that collaboration will change the world. Then it doesn't, and they think that it failed. But often the collaboration changed something - the way some part of the system works and delivers outcomes. It is a matter of understanding the nature of change itself."

*Simon Zadek is founder of AccountAbility and visiting fellow at Global Green Growth Institute, IISD and Tsinghua School of Economics and Management in Beijing. Cited in Kupers (2014).

PRINCIPLE 1:
Embrace systemic change

Human systems are complex – which means that change is dynamic and often unpredictable. This uncertainty is a basic reality that you need to take into account when engaging in MSPs. But does it mean that nothing can be planned or known? In the following, we show that some things can be known and planned. But you have to look in the right place for knowledge about the system you are trying to influence, and you have to plan together with different stakeholders, rather than at your desk.

To help you do this, we first need to introduce the concepts and language of 'complex adaptive systems'.

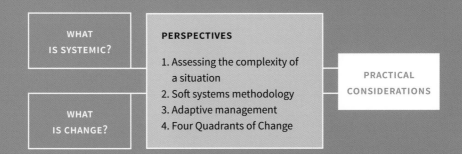

| WHAT IS SYSTEMIC? | PERSPECTIVES | PRACTICAL CONSIDERATIONS |

PERSPECTIVES

1. Assessing the complexity of a situation
2. Soft systems methodology
3. Adaptive management
4. Four Quadrants of Change

WHAT IS SYSTEMIC?

WHAT IS CHANGE?

PRACTICAL CONSIDERATIONS

Martha

Martha finally had a success: an international foundation had invited her to submit a project proposal on inclusive markets for the poor. She was director of a local NGO and had been working hard to create an alliance with business associations, producer organisations, and local government. Together, the alliance had recognised that financial risk was a critical barrier preventing farmers from linking into new market opportunities. The plan was to help drive forward local economic development supported by an innovative crop micro-insurance scheme.

But as Martha started to write the funding proposal, her heart sank. The Foundation wanted lots of detail on exactly which markets would be developed, what businesses would be involved, and which farmers would benefit. It seemed like they wanted a 'blue print' plan upfront. This type of detail and planning might be possible if you are building schools or installing water pumps, she thought to herself – but we are dealing with the uncertainty and complexity of markets and small business.

The Alliance had talked long and hard about how to stimulate the local economy and create more jobs through local enterprises, especially for youth. They realised there was no one solution, that they would need to try many different ideas, that some would work and some would fail, and that they would need to learn from this experience as they moved forward. In their analysis, the alliance had looked at the local economy as an entire system recognising the many different players and relationships. They had even drawn a 'rich picture' to visualise the complexity.

Martha realised that the Alliance, throughout all their discussions, had developed a mindset of embracing systemic change. Clearly, the Foundation had a much more linear idea of how change happens. How could she get the Foundation on board, she thought – would they be willing to join the next planning session on the micro-insurance scheme?

What do we mean by 'systemic'?

MSPs are usually about tackling challenges that are too difficult for an individual organisation to solve. These problems are called complex, difficult, or systemic. Systemic means 'in relation to the whole system'. If we have a systemic illness, it affects our entire body. Climate change is a systemic problem because it potentially impacts all aspects of the world's ecosystems and all of our social systems. Many challenges in sustainable development could be called systemic. In order to look at systemic problems, we need to think in terms of whole systems.

So what are the basic concepts of systems thinking? Imagine yourself as a 'system'. You exist in a wider environment of your family, community, and the physical surroundings. You have inputs – air, food, information – that enable you to function and produce outputs – movement, social engagement, heat, and so on. You have a whole set of sub-systems, such as your nervous system, your circulatory system, and your digestive system. These all interact, with outputs from one becoming inputs to another, controlled by a dense network of feedback mechanisms. The emergent property of all these subsystems working together is you and your particular personality, which is much more than just the sum of your parts. In systems thinking, we distinguish you from others and the wider environment by talking of a boundary.

See Section 8, Complexity and resilience

Systems can be relatively simple, with changes in inputs resulting in easily predictable changes in outputs – but they can also be highly complex, with a vast network of interrelationships. There is broad agreement among scientists that human societies are 'complex adaptive' systems. This means that they adapt and evolve in response to the combined influence of many individual agents. Nobody is in full control, and change happens in unexpected and surprising ways. This understanding has very significant implications for how to bring about social change and the role of multi-stakeholder partnerships.

Systemic ≠ systematic

Systemic refers to affecting the whole (eco)system. Systematic refers to being well organized or arranged according to a set of plan and or is grouped into systems.

Most MSPs deal with complex and 'messy' problems that have a multitude of interactions between all the different players and issues involved. It is necessary to work with this complexity, to help people see the whole system, and to recognise that change will often be an unpredictable and surprising process. A systemic approach focuses on seeing the big picture, building relationships and networks, strengthening feedback mechanisms, and adapting to the unexpected. It avoids top down 'blueprint' approaches to planning and encourages flexible, entrepreneurial, and collaborative ways of working.

There are two main ways of looking at the world around us – a reductionist way and a systems way. A reductionist approach takes things apart and breaks our understanding down into separate disciplines. Systems approaches look at how all the parts interact and what emerges from the whole system. Both approaches are needed to tackle complex problems. However, classical scientific analysis and much education has largely been reductionist. This leaves a gap in our human ability to think and act systemically. The success of MSPs hinges very much on stakeholders being able to look at their issues from a systems perspective.

Adapted from Waddell, 2011   *Types of Change*

Challenge	Simple	Complicated	Complex
Type of change	**INCREMENTAL** improving performance	**REFORM** changing the way parts interact in a system	**TRANSFORMATION** create previously unimagined possibilities
Focus	Changing ways of acting and behaving	Changing ways of thinking	Changing ways of perceiving
Core questions	How can we do more of the same?	What rules should we create?	How do I make sense out of this?
Learning loops	Single loop	Double loop	Triple loop
When to use	For routine, predictable issues	When new solutions have to be agreed upon and create previously	When no 'solution' is apparent; to innovate unimagined possibilities
Participation	Current actors addressing the problem	Stakeholders of the currently defined system	All interested in trying to understand the system
Personal role	I am acting on the problem	Others are the problem	I am part of the problem, 'we' are in this together

What do we mean by 'change'?

We all want change for the better. What drives many of us is a desire to leave the world a better place for our children, to correct wrongs, or to protect what we hold dear. We all talk about change – but what do we know about how change happens?

Significant advances have been made over recent decades in our understanding of change processes in human societies. Steve Waddell,[1] for example, distinguishes three types of change: incremental, reform, and transformation. The main features of these different types are shown in the table. Transformational change is systemic – the most difficult to achieve.

What sorts of challenge require systemic change? A typical example could be how to make the food and agriculture system sustainable – this was the starting point of the Sustainable Food Lab.[2] Meeting this challenge requires imagining things that are not yet in place, that go beyond the reform of the current system; they are certainly not about 'business as usual'

We emphasise systemic or transformational change because this is generally what is needed to address the concerns of an MSP. It isn't because we have found other types of change to be less relevant. It can be very appropriate to use tried and tested methods to solve a logistical problem with, let's say, farmer access to quality vegetable seeds. Often this type of issue can be tackled by a single organisation. But sooner or later, it becomes clear that these logistical problems are only one part of a larger system that requires innovation and new solutions: Is the lack of governance in the seed sector limiting growth? Are the seeds of today resilient enough for the impact of climate change?

These are questions requiring a systemic response. Linear approaches to project management, where all factors seem knowable and controllable, won't help you address these issues. You will need new and different methods. There is no recipe for systemic change; it emerges depending on the alignment of many circumstances – including, for example, that ordinary people keep pushing for change, often against all odds. The trick in systemic change is to recognise the relationships between the different stakeholders and circumstances, to see how these relationships can be influenced to steer the system in a desired direction.

In the following, we look at four different perspectives or ways of thinking that will help you to understand systemic change and integrate it into your MSP: assessing the complexity of a situation, the soft systems methodology, adaptive management, and the four quadrants of change.

Perspective 1: Assessing the complexity of a situation

Before thinking about systemic change, we need to understand the idea of complexity. In everyday life, we tend to think of 'complex' and 'complicated' as being more or less the same. But we can make a clearer set of distinctions that are very useful for understanding and dealing with the level of complexity in different types of situations. Dave Snowden and his colleagues have developed a decision-making framework called the Cynefin Framework[3] that distinguishes between four different types of contexts: simple,[4] complicated, complex, and chaotic. In this framework, the level of complexity is related to the nature of the relationship between cause and effect.

In simple contexts, there are limited interactions, which are all predictable. When you toggle a light switch, the same action produces the same result every time. Complicated contexts have many more parts and interactions, but they still operate in clear and predictable patterns. For instance, rockets are complicated assemblies of components, but the components interact in predictable ways; if you make a second rocket, it will behave in the same way as the first. Complex contexts, by contrast, have many elements with multiple feedback loops. This means that what happens as the result of an intervention or change can't be predicted with any certainty, although the reasons for what has happened are often apparent in retrospect. The economy is a classic example; stock markets go up and down due to many interacting factors that are largely unpredictable. In the fourth chaotic context, there is simply no relationship between cause and effect.

Cynefin Framework by Dave Snowden

COMPLEX

the relationship between
cause and effect can only be perceived
in retrospect
probe-sense-respond

EMERGENT PRACTICE

COMPLICATED

the relationship between
cause and effect requires analysis,
investigation and/or expert knowledge
sense-analyze-respond

GOOD PRACTICE

CHAOTIC

no relationship between cause
and effect at systems level
act-sense-respond

NOVEL PRACTICE

SIMPLE

the relationship between cause
and effect is obvious to all
sense-categorize-respond

BEST PRACTICE

Linear planning, and much scientific analysis, is based on identifying clear cause–effect relationships and using these to predict the outcome of a design or intervention. But in complex and chaotic contexts, you can't predict cause–effect relationships; they either cannot be assessed ahead of time or do not exist. In a complex system, behaviour emerges at the level of the system as whole; it can't be predicted by adding together the behaviour of the individual elements. Complex systems can also change suddenly. If they are close to a tipping-point, a small change in conditions can lead to a great change in the system, as happened during the global financial crisis.

Others, such as Westley, Zimmerman, and Patton[5] also make distinctions between simple, complicated, and complex tasks or problems, as shown in the table. Simple problems are straightforward and can be solved by following a standard procedure. For example, you can bake a cake by following a recipe, and as long as you follow it carefully, you can be sure of success. Complicated problems involve many more parts and may require specialist knowledge and coordination, but if all the individual steps are replicated, the outcome will be predictable. Complex problems, such as raising a child have no formulas, and what worked well with one child may not work with the next.

The three types of problems: simple, complicated, and complex, following Westley, Zimmerman and Patton

SIMPLE Baking a cake	COMPLICATED Sending a rocket to the moon	COMPLEX Raising a child
The recipe is crucial	Rigid protocols or formulas are needed	Rigid protocols have a limited application or are counter-productive
Recipes are easily replicated	Sending one rocket increases the likelihood that the next will also be a success	Raising one child provides experience but is no guarantee of success with the next
Expertise is helpful but not required	High levels of expertise in multiple fields are needed	Expertise helps, but only when balanced with responsiveness to the particular child
A good recipe produces nearly the same cake every time	Key elements of each rocket must be identical to succeed	Every child is unique and must be understood as an individual
The best recipes give good results every time	There is a high degree of certainty of outcome	Uncertainty of outcome remains

There are many things we deal with in life that are simple or complicated – but not necessarily complex. When we are building a road or bridge, we know what needs to be done, step by step, and we can make a clear plan to achieve the desired results. However, MSPs mostly involve stakeholders who are trying to tackle difficult social and institutional issues – for example, changing land tenure systems so that poor women farmers have more security and incentives to be productive. That is complex!

When trying to solve complex problems, you will need to experiment with a range of interventions to see which ones work and which ones fail – and then use this knowledge for scaling up or replicating when there is success and for trying something different when there is failure. This is essentially an evolutionary approach to managing change.

The key point is that, for different levels of complexity, we need to use different forms of analysis, planning, monitoring, and managing. The Cynefin Framework is a powerful framework that can help you – and all facilitators, leaders, and supporters of MSPs – to understand what you are dealing with, and why many classical linear approaches to analysis, problem solving, and planning have limitations in complex situations.

CDI, based on Snowden and Boone (2007)

Level of Complexity	Examples	Implications for hierarchy, control, and expertise	Implications for interventions
Simple	Constructing a village water supply	Clear command chain essential, drilling teams focus on their protocol	Can use a logframe, checklists
Complicated	Linking small-scale producers to markets	Knowledge intensive as cause and effect not self-evident	Careful planning, multiple types of expertise, logframe
Complex	Changing tax-incentives to favour small-scale producers	Politicians and battlefield commanders excel here: adaptive management; large pool of diverse expertise	Attempt many experiments; generate a lot of feedback in order to select strategies that work. Failure = learning
Chaotic	Initial response to disasters	Ideal for strong personalities who like to dictate solutions as they can take absolute control	Just act with instinct

Note: even though a problem may be very complex, parts of it can be simple - for example undertaking a research survey, setting up a website, or organising a workshop.

Perspective 2: The soft systems methodology

In order to use a systemic approach, you will first need to analyse the situation from a systems perspective. Here we draw on the soft systems methodology (SSM), developed by Peter Checkland[6] in the 1980s, to outline what this means in practice. The soft systems approach is a powerful methodology for stakeholder collaboration because it focuses thinking and discussion around inter-relationships, perspectives, and boundaries:[7]

Inter-relationships: How do things connect with each other? What are all the elements of the system (situation) you are dealing with and how do they affect each other? What will happen in the whole system if you make changes in one part? Very often stakeholders only see their part of a situation. If you can help everyone to take a wider look, this will help create shared understanding and stimulate creative thinking about what might work better.

Perspectives: What are the different ways a situation can be understood? Different stakeholders will have very different perspectives on a situation, driven in part by their own values and interests. You can use soft systems analysis to help stakeholders identify, understand, and discuss these different perspectives. You will also find that one of the critical first steps in conflict management is enabling different stakeholders to get a much deeper understanding of each other's perspectives.

Boundaries: What is 'in' and what is 'out'? When we tackle human issues, we must first decide how narrow or broad the focus should be. In other words, where do we draw the boundary between what we can try to change and what sits in the wider environment and affects us but is not easy to influence? This is an important discussion that you need to hold when developing your MSP. If you make the boundary too wide, you will be dealing with so many things that success will be difficult; if you make it too small, you may not be tackling the underlying causes of the issues. The boundaries are likely to shift during the process – this is normal. The important point is to have a conscious discussion about the scope of what the MSP is trying to tackle at any one point in time.

You can use SSM with stakeholders to develop systems models of what they will need to create an improved situation. For example, an MSP was used to design a new irrigation scheme in Nepal. Previously, planners had mainly focused on water delivery and engineering and had not paid any attention to improving agricultural practices or marketing. This meant that farmers didn't get the full benefits of the water. Systems models were then created with input from all stakeholders to show the inter-relationships between the sub-systems of water supply, agricultural production, support services, management, and marketing. A more comprehensive plan was made that helped all these areas to improve and farmers to benefit fully.

Soft systems analysis offers a number of tools to help you analyse your particular situation. Here we describe three: rich pictures, CATWOE and system diagrams.

Rich picture

One of the most powerful tools we use when facilitating MSPs is rich picturing, and this is a starting point for soft system analysis. It involves stakeholders working together to draw a picture of the situation they are concerned about. Stakeholders coming from different

Rich picture displaying a wetland management situation. Actors (donors, NGO, local government, fishermen) and factors (power issues, overfishing, conflicts, money flows) can be recognized.

backgrounds can very quickly start to see how their concerns are connected with those of others. All stakeholders can obtain a systemic overview of the situation. People enjoy working together on a rich picture; it's fun, creates lots of discussion, and often generates much laughter. The process itself helps people to understand each other's perspectives and is a great way to begin the collective analysis needed at the start of an MSP. You can learn more about how to use Rich Pictures to help stakeholders get a better (shared) insight into the system they aim to influence on CDI's MSP portal: www.mspguide.org

CATWOE

CATWOE stands for Customers, Actors, Transformation, Worldview, Owner, and Environment. You can use a CATWOE checklist to help get more clarity about the issue or goal of your MSP. Essentially, it helps you focus on the impact of the issue on the different people involved and the wider system. The checklist can be used to help identify the problem, to prompt thinking about what you are really trying to achieve, or to think about implementing a solution.

Customers	Who benefits and how does the issue affect them?
Actors	Who is involved in the situation and what roles and responsibilities do they have?
Transformation	What is the change or improvement that is desired?
World View	What is the dominant mindset that stakeholders bring to the situation?
Owner	Who owns the process? In other words, who has the power to make or stop things from happening?
Environmental	What are the environmental constraints and limitations that will impact on bringing about change?

System diagrams

The soft system methodology has a specific approach for developing conceptual models of the human activity systems required to achieve a specific purpose or transformation. For example, you could ask the question: what set of human activities would be required to improve the sustainability of tea production? You use a 'root' definition derived from CATWOE to define the overall system, and then identify the minimum number of subsystems needed for the larger system to function. This conceptual model can then be used to generate discussion with stakeholders about what changes in the 'real world' would be logically desirable and politically feasible. The full SSM analysis can be very powerful, but it is also quite sophisticated, and it would be advisable to read up on the details of how to perform it.

Example system 2: System analysis of the supply chain for a cup of tea. Source: Mulgan and Leadbeater (2013, p.12), courtesy of NESTA

If you don't want to go into the full detail of SSM, you can also work with stakeholders to develop a systems diagram of the different elements and relationships of a system, such as illustrated supply chain of tea.[8] This shows a general picture of the dynamics at play, and even if not fully analysed can clarify the opportunities for action. It shows where you can intervene and where there might be leverage.

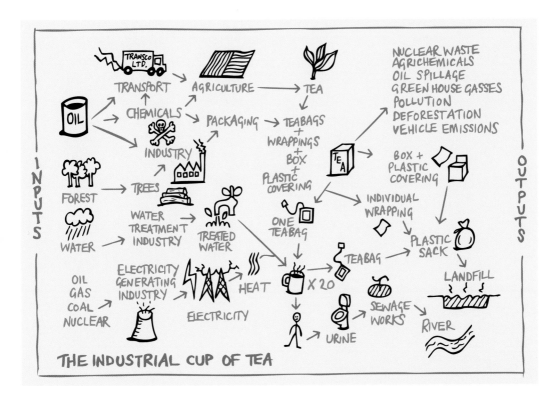

Perspective 3: Adaptive management

You will find systems analysis to be a powerful tool to help stakeholders understand the whole situation and how their actions influence others. But the very nature of complex systems is that they often change in unpredictable and surprising ways. No amount of systems analysis will overcome this. Until now, Western and scientific thought has mainly focused on the types of phenomena defined under the Cynefin Framework as simple or complicated. This leads to a classic blueprint-type planning approach that prescribes a) careful analysis, b) specifying specific outcomes or results that will be achieved, c) developing a step-by-step action plan, and d) implementing the plan. This approach assumes that, with good analysis and good planning, we will mostly succeed. But although this is largely true for simple and complicated tasks, complex and chaotic situations are different. This means that our planning approach must be adaptive – that is, responsive to what happens.

Adaptive planning uses different assumptions about change. You should assume uncertainty: that for a given situation, it just isn't possible to predict exactly what will happen when you start intervening and making changes. You should be prepared to try out lots of different ideas to see what happens, and accept that many of these ideas will fail. You should think of failure as an integral part of the innovation and change process – the basis for new learning. The trick is to carry out regular monitoring and gain rapid feedback so that you can respond quickly and adjust the approach as necessary. The different stakeholders in the MSP represent different parts of the system; when they come together, they can share their observations of what they see changing – and whether it is good or bad for them. This is a key approach for strengthening feedback and will help you to adapt your MSP planning as the situation changes.

Interested to learn more about adaptive management?
Visit CDI's portal:
www.managingforimpact.org

Adaptive planning in the seed sector in Ethiopia[9]

The seed sector in Ethiopia is complex; it involves many different stakeholders, each with their own specific role in the seed value chain. The roles include variety development, early generation seed production, seed multiplication, and seed distribution, with other stakeholders providing services such as seed quality assurance and extension. But the sector is facing many challenges in ensuring that farmers have access to quality seed.

Together, core groups of regional seed sector stakeholders, with knowledge institutes as facilitators, tried to design a process to tackle key bottlenecks in the seed value chain. The process is part of Ethiopia's Integrated Seed Sector Development (ISSD) programme. But how do you design such a process, given the complexity of the seed sector, and how do you ensure that you work towards institutional change? Trying to put principles of adaptive management into practice, the ISSD programme chose to focus on creating space to promote partnerships and innovation, rather than focusing on predefined bottlenecks and solutions.

The stakeholder platform brought together actors at different levels: the operators in the value chain (seed producers, processors, and marketers); supporters (non-governmental organisations and universities); and enablers (government agencies). This was important both for the learning process and for identifying key bottlenecks, common goals, joint interests, and mutual benefits – as well creating new partnerships. The focus on innovation led to a routine of experimentation; studies and pilots were used to find out what worked and what didn't work in improving farmers' access to quality seed. Promising innovations were validated and scaled up, and then anchored in the right institutions.

By choosing to focus on partnerships and innovation, ISSD was able to create a space for stakeholders to start working together – even though there was no predefined result. At the beginning, no one knew which innovations would stand out as being effective and scalable, and to have the potential to be included in national policies. One of the successful innovations was direct seed marketing: an institutional change that allows farmer cooperatives to sell their quality seed directly to local markets. This was only made possible by using an MSP, and planning adaptively.

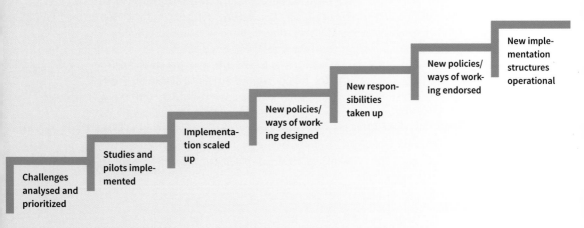

Challenges analysed and prioritized

Studies and pilots implemented

Implementation scaled up

New policies/ ways of working designed

New responsibilities taken up

New policies/ ways of working endorsed

New implementation structures operational

Perspective 4: The Four Quadrants of Change

Any change involves challenges related to the people and structures involved. You need to think about these to make sure that the change you want isn't hindered by an aspect that you didn't consider. The Four Quadrants of Change (4Q) model, developed by Ken Wilber,[10] will help you identify and address the different aspects of change. The model divides the change into four types: Quadrant 1 deals with intention, personal identity, and ways of perceiving; Quadrant 2 with behaviour and how it is developed; Quadrant 3 with culture, beliefs, and values; and Quadrant 4 with the structures and processes of social systems. Steve Waddell[11] suggests that an MSP doesn't need to lead to action in all quadrants, but should make sure that someone – its participants or others – does have interventions in all. Lack of change in one quadrant will hold up development of the others.

When you are aiming for systemic change, it is good to be aware where change begins. Does it all start with the individual choice to commit? Or do we expect that the starting point for a change of the type 'clean water and sanitation for all' is action on an institutional level? The four quadrants model will help you and your stakeholders to focus on four different strategies for change in human interactions. Working with these different strategies is another aspect of being systemic. In MSPs, this model raises important questions about how change happens and where to focus.

The change process of Dutch development NGO ICCO

Hettie Walters documented the change process in the Dutch development NGO ICCO using the Four Quadrants model[12] and a process inquiry protocol developed by the Generative Change Community.[13] ICCOs change involved moving from 'funding individual partner NGOs' to 'working with anybody who could play a role in the challenge at hand'. This shift to a multi-stakeholder mode of operation proved to be challenging, but not impossible. Reflecting on the four quadrants, ICCO learned that it had mainly focused its efforts on the exterior side of the model (How do we relate differently to our partners? How can we affect institutional change?). It did not invest enough in the internal side of the model (How do we maintain enough motivated and committed staff? How can we shape our collective aspirations for this change process?). ICCO has taken these lessons on board for managing complex change in the future.

	INTERIOR	**EXTERIOR**
INDIVIDUAL	**1. Spiritual-Psychological** Concerned with changing one's own sense of being. Broad change theory: It's all a question of individual perceptions and capacity. Focus: • Deepening self-awareness • Developing one's knowledge, skills, competencies • Describing one's assumptions, values, mindsets, beliefs Methods: • Meditation • Personal reflection and inquiry • Personal development of mastery through courses and apprenticeships	**2. Inter-Personal** Concerned with changing one's own behaviours in interaction with others. Broad change theory: It's all a question of how individuals interact. Focus: • Showing trust, respect, mutual understanding • Shifting behaviours to demonstrate interdependence • Reaching conciliation of inter-personal differences Methods: • Diversity training • Learning journeys into other people's worlds • Group encounters/retreats for exploration • Mediation/negotiations training
COLLECTIVE	**3. Social and Cultural** Concerned with collective values of fairness and justice. Broad change theory: It's all a question of collective values and beliefs. Focus: • Collective goals and aspirations • Underlying values and beliefs • Implicit 'rules' and assumptions • Discourse, language Methods: • Collective goal-setting and strategy creation • Developing value statements and processes for actualization • On-going media programmes	**4. Structural and Systemic** Concerned with governance, decision-making processes and institutions. Broad change theory: It's all a question of processes, institutions and power. Focus: • Policies, legislation • Institutions, procedures • Allocation of resources Methods: • Building political structures, agreements, frameworks, systems • New accounting/reporting/measurement systems

Source: Steve Waddell (2011, p 106) and the Generative Change Community (2007), adapted from Wilber (2000)

Practical implications

Acting systemically means aligning change processes with the way in which complex adaptive systems evolve. What does this mean for you and your MSP?

· Don't expect things to go as planned. Design processes around multiple cycles of reflection, planning, and action, so that you can adapt your plans to unexpected change.

· Recognise that, in complex systems, change happens because of the actions of many different actors. Build a broad network of support and be wary of centralised and top-down approaches.

· Don't put all your eggs in one basket; try out a range of options to discover what works best.

· Be entrepreneurial and look for and support the emerging successes that could be triggers for fundamental, systemic change.

· Expect and learn from failure. In the evolution of complex systems, there is much failure and just a few big successes that change the system.

Remember:

· You need to get 'the system in the room' by bringing different stakeholders together and supporting them to share their different perspectives.

· You must carry out regular reviews and adaptation of any change strategy; the dynamics in complex systems will change quickly and are unpredictable.

· MSPs do best when they allow for experimentation, prototyping, and learning. Donors should see these investments as musts, not 'nice-to-haves'.

· MSPs need to consider systemic change as something that they can contribute to, and not as something they can fully control and steer.

Questions for designing and facilitating MSPs

· How complex are the issues you are dealing with? Will a linear approach to planning work, or do stakeholders need to engage in a more adaptive approach to change?

· What are the mindsets of the different stakeholders involved? Do they understand the difference between linear and adaptive approaches, and how could they be helped to accept and use a systemic approach?

· What are the different ways in which this situation can be understood? How will this understanding affect the way in which people judge the success of the MSP?

PRINCIPLE 2:
Transform institutions

When we talk about social, economic, and political change, we are really talking about changing the underlying institutions or traditions. By 'institutions' we mean the 'rules of the game', the formal and informal norms and values that shape how people think and behave. Deeply held values, established traditions, and formal frameworks can be real barriers to change, but they can also be supportive and help you to achieve your aims. MSPs need to help stakeholders look critically at the institutions – their own and those of others – that affect their work.

This section is all about helping you to recognise, understand, and work with the institutions that may support or hinder the success of your MSP. There are ways to use MSPs to influence institutions to move in a desirable direction – but it takes time.

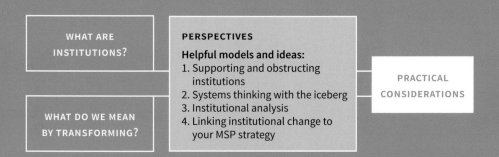

WHAT ARE INSTITUTIONS?

WHAT DO WE MEAN BY TRANSFORMING?

PERSPECTIVES
Helpful models and ideas:
1. Supporting and obstructing institutions
2. Systems thinking with the iceberg
3. Institutional analysis
4. Linking institutional change to your MSP strategy

PRACTICAL CONSIDERATIONS

Albert

When Albert returned from his field trip, his mind was buzzing with impressions of the nutrition programme. He should leave his bilateral donor office more often. All these new SMS-based health applications, public outreach through radio and mobile, new technologies for food storage... impressive!

But one comment from a woman farmer still bothered him. "They can say what they want about this new variety of rice, I am never going to feed it to my family. It can't be good." The whole programme was built on the idea that the new variety was better, tastier, and more nutritious. It had been proven in other countries. Why was there so much resistance here?

Was there something cultural they had missed? Why was it so hard to for people to see the benefits of new proven technology? What could he do to help things change?

What do we mean by 'institutions'?

When we talk about institutions, we don't mean organisations; we mean the 'rules' that help society to function. These can be formal or informal; they can be political, legal, social, cultural, economic, or religious. In the widest sense, institutions include language, currency, marriage, property rights, taxation, education, and laws. Institutions help us know how to behave in given situations, such as driving in traffic, bargaining at a market, or attending a wedding.

Institutions are critical for establishing trust in society. We put our money in a bank because we trust the institutions of the financial system to protect it. We board an airplane because we trust the institutions related to air traffic control and monitoring of aircraft maintenance to keep us safe.

By definition, institutions are stable, long lasting, and resist change. Institutions can even lock societies into a particular path. Try to imagine how difficult it would be to change the convention of driving on the right or left side of the road now that it's established.

The different institutions that govern our lives are interrelated in a complex network. The rules of language make it possible for laws to be established, these laws are upheld by courts and policing systems, and we obey the laws because of a whole system of societal beliefs, values and norms. Our lives are embedded in this complex web of social institutions. We take many of them for granted, not questioning their origin or the underlying assumptions and beliefs on which they are based. Informal institutions usually evolve without conscious planning, and become embedded in our idea of 'normal'. This means that it is much easier for us to recognise other people's institutions than to understand our own. The ideas and attitudes can be so deeply embedded in our way of thinking that we find the idea of change very unsettling.

Formal versus Informal

If you have ever been to Amsterdam, you may know that traffic is regulated through traffic lights. Traffic control is a formal institution, known to everybody. But many visitors are surprised to see that cyclists often ignore these rules and happily cycle through a red light. It seems there is an informal institution at work ('if it's clear, you can cross'), which is different from the formal institution ('you must always stop at red traffic lights').

What do we mean by transforming?

You will know from your own experience how tough it can be to change institutions. But it is likely to be an important step in achieving the aim of an MSP. We are not suggesting that MSPs can always or easily change institutions in the short term. Institutional change can take generations (think of attitudes towards the role of marriage) and often involve patient battles by many brave people. In general, institutions change slowly with incremental steps, although sometimes a new technological innovation might have a rapid impact (for example, the invention of mobile payment technology on the institution of banking).

If you want your MSP to be effective, you need to understand which institutions are hindering change – even if changing them is difficult – and which are needed to support it. You will need to pay focused and sustained attention to the institutions that are most important – not try to do everything at once. Through MSPs, you have the potential to influence more institutions because you can leverage the collective power and intelligence of many stakeholders.

See Section 4, Principle 1: Embrace systemic change

Sometimes, a small change in an institution can have a huge effect. This is because we are working with complex adaptive systems, as explained in Principle 1. When the system is close to a tipping point, small interventions can have huge consequences. Consider the proverbial straw that breaks the camel's back, or the events that led up to the fall of the Berlin Wall. The box gives another example in a development context.

Perspective 1: Enabling and constraining factors

It can be hard to grasp the concept of institutions because they are so integrated in our lives that we often don't notice them. One of the easiest ways to think about the role that institutions can play in achieving the goals of your MSP is to separate them into two types:
1. Those that will enable your MSP to reach its ultimate goal
2. Those that will hinder or constrain your MSP from reaching its ultimate goal

As an example, your MSP might be concerned with providing access to clean drinking water. Start by listing all the institutions that are enablers for this goal, such as having a national legal framework and strong community solidarity. Then list all the constraining institutions, such as a culture of corruption in the public sector or women not being allowed to leave the house. Which are the most important? Try to put each list in order of priority. Your list of enablers will help you see where you can get support for your MSP goals. And your list of constraints will help you decide where you should start a process of change.

Finding out which underlying institutions are playing a role will help you to develop your Theory of Change with the stakeholders.

See Section 2: Designing Processes, for more on ToC

Nepal: reducing land degradation by institutionalising leasehold groups*

This box gives an example of how a relatively small institutional change contributed to big impact.

Land degradation in the hill areas of Nepal has been a huge problem since the 1990s, as more people cut down trees for firewood, leading to bare slopes, erosion, and decline of agricultural productivity. The government had tried all kinds of agro-ecological approaches to prevent forests from disappearing, and some (like community forestry) have become quite successful in stopping the decline. But how could the damaged land be repaired? Finally, someone came up with the idea of leasing the degraded forest land to poor farmers, which was taken up by the government with support from FAO and IFAD. Although poor people couldn't buy land, having a long-term lease gave them all kinds of possibilities. This small institutional change – introducing a legal framework for leasing – was a game changer. The government granted leaseholds on the degraded forest land tax-free to eligible poor families, and provided training and some inputs. The leasehold groups were put in charge of protecting the land from grazing and fire. They could use the land for natural regeneration of forest or for agroforestry with plantations of multipurpose trees and crops. Forest coverage increased by up to 70% in ten years. And the leasehold families could now pay for schooling, health, and daily family expenses with the income from the land.

*See IFAD evaluations of the Nepal leasehold forestry programme: http://tinyurl.com/on64e6k

Perspective 2: Systems thinking with the iceberg

It can be very difficult to unpack the particular situation that your MSP is facing. You can see what is happening, but it can be really challenging to identify the different influences and institutions that led to the situation. The more formal institutions – say, laws that limit exports – can be easy to see. But why don't people in your village trust a new product even when it works better? What led to the cyclists in Amsterdam ignoring red lights: A culture that favours cyclists? Respect for personal decision making? A culture of low enforcement by police? Many different institutions may play a role. Before you try to change the situation, you will need to have some understanding of the patterns, structures, and attitudes that created it.

There are many ways of trying to analyse the situation, but one tool that people have found very useful is the 'Iceberg'.[14] This tool, developed by Reos Partners, helps us to look at how the whole system functions. The iceberg illustrates how much lies below what you directly observe. You can only see directly the part that is above the waterline – one tenth of the whole.

The real mass lies below the surface. In a system, the events that you see are just one indication of the patterns that are in place. The patterns have evolved on the basis of various structures and the whole is supported by particular ways of thinking, mental models[15] that exist in society and within individuals. The mental models include the norms and values of our society and social groups as we discussed at the start of this section. These ways of thinking are persistent, but they are also the most hidden part of the iceberg, we may even be unaware that they exist. The mass of the system that you don't consciously see – the part below the surface – is what gives institutions their stability.

Events	What happend?
Patterns	What's been happening?
Structures	What might explain the events/patterns?
Mental models	How does our thinking allow this situation to persist?

Real transformation in MSPs doesn't usually come because of a new event, or a change in behaviour. It happens when we can shift the mental models that gave birth to the event or behaviour. Different stakeholder groups often have different mental models, and these shape their understanding and the decisions they make. It is essential to create situations that help the stakeholders in your MSP to talk to each other and to find out where and why their thinking differs. Often stakeholders then explore their different mental models and those of others involved in the process. Once the stakeholders in the MSP understand the different mental models involved, they can think about which models are useful and which need to change, including their own. New mental models may even emerge that everyone shares.

Perspective 3: A framework for institutional analysis

What other ways are there to analyse institutions? Institutions are linked in a complex pattern, and you may find it really difficult to understand which ones are involved, and how they are influencing your particular situation. The different perspectives described in the previous paragraphs will help, but you may need to know more. And you need to understand how the institutions interact. It is easy to find tools for stakeholder, problems and power analysis, but there is no widely accepted framework for analysing institutions.[16]

See Section 6: Tools

In many fields, whether education, market access, health, or the environment, you will be looking at a messy web of many interacting institutions, not just one. We have developed a framework[17] to help you ask critical questions about the institutions affecting your situation and how they interact. The basic outline is shown graphically in the figure. The framework deliberately takes a very broad perspective. We divide the institutions into four basic domains: 'meaning', 'association', 'control', and 'action'. Each has two subdivisions, which reflects the idea of including both formal and informal institutions. Formal and informal institutions are equally important, and often reinforce each other. The institutions connect with each other in different ways; together they structure our social interactions.

Framework for exploring the complexity of institutions

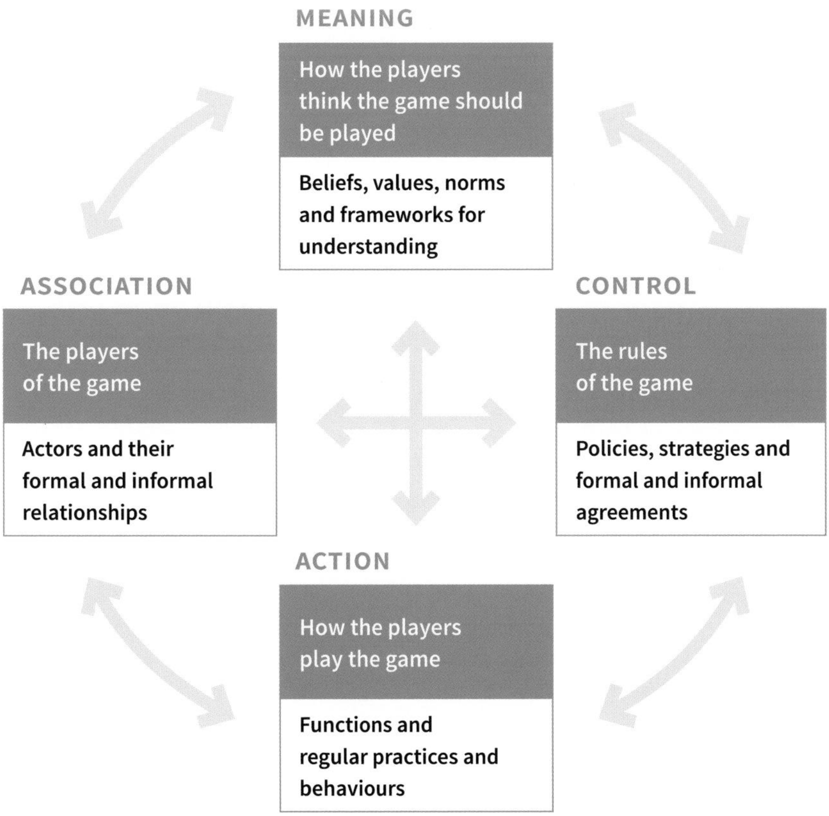

MEANING

How the players think the game should be played

Beliefs, values, norms and frameworks for understanding

ASSOCIATION

The players of the game

Actors and their formal and informal relationships

CONTROL

The rules of the game

Policies, strategies and formal and informal agreements

ACTION

How the players play the game

Functions and regular practices and behaviours

The table shows the types of institutions found in the different domains – with some examples to give you a feel for the range covered by the idea of 'institution'. There are institutions based on ideas or meaning, institutions that are associations of people, institutions developed to regulate or control how our society functions, and institutions to do with how we act. It's important to ask questions about the whole range of factors that may be causing the people involved in your MSP to behave in a particular way.

Using the framework for institutional analysis: the example of food safety*

We can illustrate some of the different types and interactions of institutions by looking at issues around food quality and safety. Consumer beliefs ('meaning') – perhaps about the health risks of genetically modified organisms – and buying behaviour ('action') help shape business strategy and government policy making ('control'). Regulations and procedures have been developed for food quality and safety ('control') based on a framework for scientific understanding and research ('meaning'). Government agencies have been formed to oversee food safety issues, and businesses have been set up for buying, selling, and processing at different points along the value chain ('association'). Government food safety agencies are mandated to develop policies and establish rules and regulations, while the agrifood industry independently develops its own policies, standards, and rules to meet consumer demands and legal requirements ('control'). These arrangements lead to formal types of supporting actions, such as regular monitoring of imports by a food safety authority or bar coding and tracing by agribusiness ('action'). Some behaviours ('action'), for example corruption or direct sales to friends, may be driven by informal customs and rules ('control') that disregard the formal arrangements.

*Vermeulen et al (2008)

Type	Description	Examples
MEANING		
Beliefs and values	The underlying and often deeply held assumptions on which people base decisions	• Assumptions about human nature • Beliefs about why some people are poor and others are rich • Beliefs about how much governments should intervene in markets • Business values that further corruption or social responsibility • Religious beliefs and values
Frameworks for understanding	Language, theories, and concepts used to communicate, explain phenomena, and guide action	• Language • Economic theory • Principles of law and democratic governance
ASSOCIATION		
Organisations and networks	Organisations created by government, business, and civil society	• Government agencies • Industry associations, small business associations • NGO coalitions, producer organisations • Religious organisations
Relationships and transactions	The ways and means for building and maintaining relationships between individuals and among organisations	• Markets • Global economic forum • Business lunches, alumni meetings
CONTROL		
Mandates, policies and strategies	The mandates given or taken by particular groups and organisations, the positions and policies they adopt and the strategies they try to follow	• National constitutions • Global conventions • Government policies/ national poverty-reduction strategies • Corporate strategy for socially responsible entrepreneurship • NGO position on genetically modified organisms (GMOs)
Formal and informal rules	The formal and informal rules that set the constraints for how organisations and individuals can behave in given situations	• Traffic rules and regulations • Accepted form of wedding ceremonies • Laws on treatment of employees • Environmental regulations
ACTION		
Functions, products and services	The functions carried out and products and services delivered by government, private, and civil society organisations	• Tax collection and administration • Extension, health, and education services • Financial services provided by banks • Provision of infrastructure by government
Regular practices and behaviours	The practices and behaviours that individuals repeat in social, economic, and political life	• Individual shopping patterns • Normal behaviour of people in markets • How people greet each other • How public servants interact with the public

Perspective 4: Linking institutional change to your MSP strategy

You cannot change institutions overnight. The rules that have developed are very persistent and may take generations to shift. Think, for example, of how long it takes to really change an institution that doesn't support minority rights, or has gender-based discrimination woven into its fabric. But don't be disheartened: even if an MSP cannot bring about change instantly, it can start the process and have a real impact – as long as you have analysed carefully what is happening, and target the institutions that are really driving or blocking your issue. The case in Ghana described in the box will give you an idea of an approach used by one MSP to start addressing institutional constraints.

Not waiting for the elite to tell us what to do

There is a lot of illegal logging taking place in Ghana, and the loss of forest is affecting people's sense of wellbeing, as well as harming the environment. Although there are regulations, people are not following them. Ghana's Forestry Commission and Forestry Research Institute started a multi-stakeholder dialogue to address conflict and illegality in the domestic timber market.

Establishing this dialogue showed their shared commitment to adjusting the way policy was made in the forest sector. Until now, everyone had waited for central government to define the problem, develop a policy, and inform those affected – a conventional command-and-control approach. Now the organisations faced with the problems on the ground had decided to start the policy development process themselves, and then involve other stakeholders, including central government.

This meant that the practitioners could define their own policy objectives, instead of the objectives being set solely by the governing elite (industry, politicians). In this way, they seriously questioned the legitimacy of the conventional rules. Until now, forest policy had been decided by the powerful and industry experts on their own; now the discussion had moved to a new space where all stakeholders could discuss at the same table. (Source: James Parker Mckeown et al 2013[18])

There are many other examples we can give of how people in MSPs have worked towards changing existing institutions. Some have focused on individual action and leadership to end a harmful practice (such as gender discrimination). Others have used technological innovation to change the accepted system. Mobile technology is a classic example. In Kenya, M-PESA was able to challenge the existing rules and regulations on financial services by inventing mobile banking. Banks had dominated the financial services for years, but now new technology, combined with a lot of stakeholder negotiation, helped to rewrite the rules of the game.[19] In only 5 years, this led to 83% of the adult population in Kenya having access to mobile money,[20] giving them more control over their assets and helping them transform their lives.

It is important to keep in mind that institutions can support the change you want to create as well as constrain it. If you identify a supportive institution, then help it to have even more influence on people's behaviours. If you identify a constraining institution, then focus your strategy on reducing its impact, and adjusting it in the long run. In both situations, you should discuss honestly with your stakeholders how much influence the MSP can really have. Don't focus your energies on something that is bound to fail. In fact, most innovation happens at the fringes of a system – not at the very centre, as Achi and Garvey Berger[21] argue: "We can give up the hunt for the root cause and instead look to the edges of an issue for our experiments. The system's centre is most resistant to change, but tinkering at the periphery can deliver outsized returns".

Finally, remember that some 'rules of the game' will be replicated in your MSP. All stakeholders in the MSP have their own implicit values and norms, which will be brought into the dialogue. We saw a very good example when working with a group of NGOs that were trying to set up MSPs to shift the balance of power between civil society, government, and the private sector. The NGOs were very aware of power issues and understood the processes involved; this was what they were working on. But the coalition almost fell apart because of an internal power struggle between the NGO directors. They could understand how to work on issues of power with others, but didn't recognise what was happening in their own situation. Here we helped the NGOs to reflect on their own rules of the game (gaining power at any cost so they could ensure the 'best' outcome) before they could start useful discussions with government and the private sector.

See Principle 3: Work with power

Practical implications

· Remember that there are many
  different types of institutions,
  formal and informal, on many
  levels.

· Help stakeholders question their
  own 'rules of the game' (norms
  and values) and the effect they may
  have on the changes they want to
  bring about.

· Bring stakeholders together to
  discuss and analyse critically the
  institutions that may enable or
  block the changes the MSP wants
  to bring about.

· Recognise that changing
  institutions is a long-term process.

Questions for designing and facilitating MSPs

· Which are the key constraining
  institutions for your MSP? How can
  you change them or reduce them?

· Which are the key supportive
  institutions? How can you build on
  them? Strengthen them?

· What is the scope of your MSP
  – which institutions can you
  influence, which can't you?

· What other stakeholders do you
  need to bring on board to make
  the MSP work in the light of this
  institutional context?

PRINCIPLE 3:
Work with power

Power is something we see and experience every day. We tend to notice it most when it prevents us doing something we want to do, or leads to changes that we don't like. But power isn't just a negative force as we sometimes think; it can also be used to bring about positive change. When you try to change something, you may find that power differences and power abuse stand in the way, and it can be important to try to influence powerful stakeholders to shift power structures in the right direction. Equally, empowering particular stakeholder groups – helping them get into a position where they can use power constructively – can be key to developing equitable multi-stakeholder change processes. Using power positively means harnessing the maximum leverage to achieve change. The following is all about what you can do to understand and influence power structures so that they work for, and not against, the goals of your MSP.

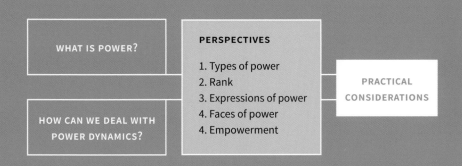

WHAT IS POWER?

HOW CAN WE DEAL WITH POWER DYNAMICS?

PERSPECTIVES

1. Types of power
2. Rank
3. Expressions of power
4. Faces of power
4. Empowerment

PRACTICAL CONSIDERATIONS

"Why do you think you'll get invited to the meeting, Kelly? The door will be closed as always". Her friend James was right: it was a bit unrealistic to think that a small NGO would be able to influence the big players in land governance. The announcement showed that three Ministries would be present, the World Bank of course, and a range of donors and their academic consultants.

Yet the topic they were discussing was how land grab could be prevented, and this was precisely what Kelly's NGO was trying to do. It helped organise people who had been thrown off their land because some high-up person had decided the land belonged to someone else. The people Kelly worked with had a stake in this issue – they were seriously affected.

But how could Kelly get connected to this seemingly impenetrable stronghold?"

What do we mean by 'power'?

People often think about power as something that constrains, or that others use in a coercive or dominating way. But power is also the means for achieving your goals. Power is neither inherently bad nor inherently good: what matters is how it is used, and towards what end.

Power is what enables any individual or organisation to bring about change. Power structures in society can also 'lock-in' patterns of behaviour, ideas and beliefs, and privileges and inequalities. MSPs aim to harness the different powers of stakeholders to bring about a change that is in everyone's interest. So, dealing with power is central to any MSP, and you need to understand power and know how to use it for change.

How can we deal with power dynamics?

Power, politics, institutions, and conflict are closely related. Institutional arrangements (See Principle 2 Adjusting Institutions) can lead to particular groups having particular power. Politics is the 'game' of using the power you have to bring about the change you would like – while protecting your interests. The use and misuse of power is often a key source of conflict.

At CDI, people often ask us about the best way to deal with power dynamics when working with multiple stakeholders. We usually answer by giving three ideas to consider:
1) Everyone has some sort of power – and change starts by becoming aware of the power involved.
2) It is not easy to redistribute power in an MSP in order to level the playing field, but there are ways you can work towards it.
3) Don't be naive about power. If the MSP is about real and different interests, you will need to be politically adept; don't underestimate what people will do to protect their interests.

In the following, we look at five different perspectives that will help you understand power and how you can work with it in your MSP: types of power; rank; expressions of power; the hidden, visible, and invisible faces of power; and empowerment in an MSP.

We define power

as the ability of actors to achieve their goals. People have power of different types, from different sources, and in different spaces. Power is not an absolute, and power shifts are possible.

Perspective 1: Types of power

There are many different ways of describing and categorising power. The classic study published by French and Raven in 1959[22] describes five forms of power, later expanded to six:

- **Coercive power:** the use of physical violence or psychological manipulation to control what others do
- **Legitimate power:** the formal or informal authority given to or taken by a particular individual or group; for example governments, legal systems, managers in organisations, and leadership of social groups
- **Reward power:** the access to and control over financial and material resources; includes the ability to give rewards to others such as money, benefits, time off, gifts, and promotions
- **Referent power:** the use of ideas, culture, religion and language to shape the way people see their world and behave (ideological), and the ability of an individual to use the power of their personality to gain a following and influence (charismatic)
- **Expert power:** the power people derive from their skills, knowledge, and experience; only applies to the speciality area of the expert
- **Informational power:** power resulting from the possession of knowledge that others need or want; the way in which information is used – sharing it, keeping it secret from key people, organising it, increasing it, or even falsifying it – can create a shift in power within a group

Looking at these types of power, it is clear that institutions and individuals – whether in government, NGOs, businesses, or as private citizens – have access to and control over, or are excluded from, different types of power. Think about any dictatorial person you know: they are likely to use different types of power to consolidate their position. Or think about an effective manager, and how they tap into different types of power to get their team to achieve great results.

Perspective 2: Rank

See Section 6, Tool 30: Power ranking

Another concept that can help you understand how power operates is rank, or 'the sum of a person's privileges'. At CDI, we often prepare people for their roles in MSPs by reflecting on their rank. As explained by Arnold Mindell, rank describes how influential someone is in the hierarchy of a group. In other words, it is the level of an individual's social or personal power. People derive their rank from various sources:

- **Situational rank:** for example, position in an organisation
- **Social rank:** for example, gender, educational level, age, race
- **Personal rank:** for example, charismatic, insecure, avoiding conflict
- **Spiritual rank:** for example, feeling connected to something transcendental, knowing your calling in life

Interestingly, people often do not know that they have a particular rank. We tend to focus on ways of decreasing the rank of those with more power instead of focusing on ways to increase our own rank. Becoming aware of how rank affects you and others is the first step in understanding the subtle power dynamics operating among stakeholders in an MSP.

How power can shift

The facilitator of a seaweed value chain in the Philippines used a stakeholder meeting to reflect on the issue of power. Less powerful stakeholders, such as the seaweed farmers, were completely surprised when the head of the provincial police spoke up saying that he felt powerless in addressing illegal fishing along the coast. The police would arrest perpetrators, but would then receive phone calls from higher up ordering their release. Corruption in the government system caused even the police to feel the limits of their power. Knowing this immediately shifted the balance in the value chain, because the seaweed farmers realized they were not the only ones being overruled and excluded. This empowered them to work proactively with the other stakeholders to negotiate better terms for their produce.

Source: Hiemstra, Brouwer and van Vugt (2012)

Perspective 3: Expressions of power

Another approach that can help you to understand how power works is to think about the four expressions of power – power over, power with, power to, and power within – which is based on the ideas in the book A New Weave of Power, People & Politics by VeneKlasen and Miller.[23]

The first, power over, is often thought of as the negative and coercive expression of power, with domination or control of one person, group, or institution over another. The three other expressions of power pave the way for a more positive line of thinking.

Expression	What does it mean in practice?
Power over: domination or control	This can be brute force or authority, but it can also be exercised by influencing what others think they can do.
Power to: individual ability to act	This is rooted in the belief that every individual has the 'power to' make a difference.
Power with: collective action, the ability to act together	'Power with' helps build bridges across different interests, experiences and knowledge and is about bringing together resources and strategies.
Power within: individual or collective sense of self-worth, value, dignity	Enhancing the 'power within' of individuals builds their capacity to imagine and helps raise aspirations on change.

The to, with, and within forms of power are sometimes called 'agency'. People working in development programmes often try to foster these forms of power. When developing an MSP, you should try to avoid relying on power over tactics, and focus on using power to, with, and within more effectively.

Perspective 4: The hidden, visible, and invisible faces of power

One of the most widely used ways of analysing power in political decision making and democratic participation looks at the three faces or dimensions of visible, hidden, and invisible. The following summary, adapted from A New Weave of Power, People and Politics,[24] draws on the theoretical work of Stephen Lukes and John Gaventa.

• **Visible power:** observable decision-making. Visible power describes the formal rules, structures, authorities, institutions, and procedures of political decision-making. It also describes how those in positions of power use such procedures and structures to maintain control. Examples: elections, political parties, budget, laws

- **Hidden power:** setting the political agenda. Powerful actors also maintain influence by controlling who gets to the decision-making table and what gets on the agenda. These dynamics operate on many levels, often excluding and devaluing the concerns and representation of less powerful groups. Examples: consultation processes that exclude some voices; and setting the agenda behind the scene.
- **Invisible power:** shaping meaning and what is acceptable. Invisible power shapes the psychological and ideological boundaries of participation. Significant problems and issues are not only kept from the decision-making table, but also from the minds and consciousness of those affected. This level of power shapes people's beliefs, sense of self, and acceptance of the status quo by influencing how individuals think about their place in the world. Processes of socialisation, culture, and ideology perpetuate exclusion and inequality by defining what is normal, acceptable, and safe. Example: negative stereotypes that limit the roles of certain groups.

VeneKlasen and Miller also summarise some strategies for responding to each of these faces of power:

- Responding to **visible power** is usually about trying to change the who, how, and what of policy-making so that the process becomes more democratic, accountable, and responsive to diverse needs. You can attempt to counter visible power by using strategies of political advocacy and seeking access to formal decision-making processes.
- Responding to **hidden power** focuses on strengthening organisations and movements of the poor and marginalised, building collective power and leadership to redefine the political agenda, and raising the visibility and legitimacy of issues, voices, and demands that have been silenced.
- Responding to **invisible power** focuses on re-imagining the social and political culture. By raising awareness, you can help transform the way people perceive themselves and those around them, and how they envisage future possibilities and alternatives.

It is often easier to engage with visible and hidden power than with power that is embedded in cultural and social norms and practices. But if you ignore invisible power, you are likely to misread the complex ways in which change happens and to find it harder to identify the best change strategies.

These three dimensions of power are not only exercised from above (power over). They can be exercised from below in the form of resistance and as expressions of power to, power with, or power within. Some citizen's groups may be able to mobilise their own forms of hidden or invisible power as a strategy for empowerment and social change.

Perspective 5: Empowerment in an MSP[25]

In order to help your MSP work more effectively, you may need to look at ways of empowering particular stakeholder groups so that they can contribute on an equal footing with the others. It sounds easy – empowerment by building capacity and building confidence. But in practice, it is very hard; you need a combination of creating space and keeping out of the way. The most effective approach is to design processes in which the less powerful stakeholders can do their own analysis and define their own strategies and plans, instead of having someone do it for them.

See Perspective 3: Expressions of Power

This means that we first need to ask questions about the people or groups concerned with empowering others. Where do they get their power from? Why are they in the business of empowering others? Robert Chambers added a fifth expression of power to the four of power over, power with, power to, and power within – the 'power to empower others'. He sees this as critical to development thinking and practice. And he emphasises that those with power cannot disown it, but should instead accept it quietly and focus on using their power sensitively and meaningfully to empower others.

At CDI we often come across MSPs where one stakeholder group is underrepresented, not invited, or doesn't speak the specialist jargon well enough to engage effectively. In such cases, you may find it appropriate to organise parallel or preceding activities with this group which focus on building capacity, filling in knowledge gaps, formulating strategies, and increasing confidence, so that the group can, at a later stage, make a more meaningful and effective contribution to the MSP. We call this a 'partisan MSP' as it is about organising an element of the system, instead of the full system. The MSP can derive considerable benefit from aligning positions and building capacities among likeminded stakeholders before engaging the full range of stakeholders. Other participants may feel that the facilitator is 'taking sides' by focusing on one group, but when we explain that this will benefit the larger MSP, they usually accept the process. If some of the stakeholders are excluded or bypassed because they don't have the capacity to engage, then the MSP may lose legitimacy. Stakeholders who are not being recognised eventually become disenfranchised, and there is a real risk that the solutions the MSP finds to the issue at hand will become unsustainable.

Very importantly it is not just differences in power between stakeholder groups that need to be considered, but also power differences within.
Are women able to speak up and participate in decision making?
Do some individuals dominate the views of the stakeholder group?
It is critical to think about all the different actors and groups and how they are able to voice their perspectives and interests in the MSP process.
(For further information on gender, see KIT, AgriProFocus and IIRR (2012) and http://genderinvaluechains.ning.com)

We also need to explore what it means to lack power. One way of doing this is to use the type of framework often used in gender analysis to learn how women and men experience power in the public, private, and intimate spaces of their lives. These realms of power are frequently ignored in power analysis, but the same framework can be used to look at the way in which different groups experience power differently. As summarised by VeneKlasen and Miller,

- the **public** realm of power concerns your experience of public interactions in areas such as employment, livelihoods, market activities, public social spaces, and the community;
- the **private** realm of power includes your experience of family, relationships, friends, marriage, and the household, which is often defined by social, cultural and religious norms; and
- the **intimate** realm of power concerns personal self-esteem, confidence, dignity, the relationship to your own body, reproductive health, and sexuality.

We can look at the case of a young professional woman as an example. This woman may be respected in her place of work, but lack status in her home or community. Or she may have power at home but be marginalised in the public realm. Similarly, she may feel powerful in the public or private realms, but not in the intimate realm; and her lack of power in the intimate or private realms may serve to undermine her sense of power in the public realm.

Thinking about the public, private, and intimate realms of power, will help you to look at the ways in which experiences in particular spaces are shaped by, and reinforce, gender and other socially constructed norms. A person's sense of identity and power as defined by gender, age, ethnicity, religion, or sexuality may shift from moment to moment according to the realm that they are in.

This framework sheds light on personal and familial sources of power, which are often ignored – even though everyone experiences them. MSPs often call for stakeholders to leave their comfort zones and engage with other, possibly unfamiliar, stakeholders. Remember that you may need to help people feel at ease in this new realm of power, so that they can make an effective contribution to the MSP.

Practical implications

Power dynamics will play a central role in any MSP, and how you deal with them will influence the levels of trust, openness, and overall legitimacy of the process. This means that it is critical to unpack the power dynamics and to seek to understand them. There are five main points you should consider when looking at the best way to deal with power plays in an MSP.

· Change the power dynamics. Bringing about transformative change means that you need to tackle the underlying issues that have created power differences. This doesn't necessarily mean a large-scale action: it could be as simple as giving small-scale farmers access to information about market prices so that they can avoid being exploited by traders. You need to understand the changes the MSP is trying to enable in terms of shifting power relations and in terms of the power needed to create change.

· Harness the power that you have. MSPs need to harness the power that the participating stakeholders have and direct it effectively. For this, you need to understand who has what power, and how this power can be used strategically and coherently to support the desired change.

· Manage the inevitable power plays. You need to manage power plays in an MSP in a way that preserves the legitimacy of the process. If people have genuinely different interests, and no one wants to compromise, conflict can become dominant and block the change the MSP is trying to achieve. Be careful that powerful groups don't capture the MSP and further disadvantage already disempowered stakeholders.

· Allow for prior work with less influential stakeholders. You may need to work with less influential stakeholder groups and individuals ('partisan' stakeholder processes) to build their sense of empowerment before they can participate meaningfully and take part in a dialogue with those who normally have power over them. Similarly, you may need to work with more privileged groups to build their willingness to share and delegate power, to help ensure that they can make a constructive contribution to the process.

· Language matters when discussing power. Stakeholders who have a lot of power in an MSP usually don't like to talk about power because they fear losing it. But stakeholders who lack power often want to put it on the agenda. Putting power on the agenda doesn't usually help to improve the power balance. It can be better not to use the word power – even when it is the elephant in the room. Try using different words (like talking about politics or each person's unique contribution) and choose appropriate timing – wait until initial trust has been built. This will help you to guide a constructive conversation about power.

Questions for designing and facilitating MSPs

· What kinds of power do you use and rely on in different relationships in your life?

· What kinds of power do others use over or with you?

· What forms of power play a role in the change your MSP is trying to bring about? How can the MSP best influence these power dynamics?

· What types of power do the different stakeholders bring into your MSP? How can these powers be harnessed and used?

· Do the powers and influence of particular stakeholder groups mean that their interests and views could dominate the process? How can you help create more equity?

· How can you strengthen the power of marginalised or disadvantaged groups so that they can be better represented in the process and play a more effective role?

PRINCIPLE 4:
Deal with conflict

Conflict is an inevitable and normal part of any multi-stakeholder process. We talk about conflict when parties or individuals have genuinely different interests and struggle over them, rather than negotiating between them. Conflict can also be necessary and desirable for change to occur. Thus understanding, surfacing, and dealing with conflict is an essential step in developing an effective MSP. In the following, we offer you some ways of understanding and dealing with conflict.

"All societies, communities, organisations, and interpersonal relationships experience conflict at one time or another in the process of day-to-day interaction. Conflict is not necessarily bad, abnormal, or dysfunctional: it is a fact of life" - Moore, 1986

| WHAT IS CONFLICT? | PERSPECTIVES | PRACTICAL CONSIDERATIONS |

WHAT IS CONFLICT?

PERSPECTIVES

1. Causes of conflict
2. Continuum of conflict
3. Interest-based negotiation

PRACTICAL CONSIDERATIONS

WHAT DOES 'DEALING WITH' MEAN?

"We must avoid conflict at all cost", Lanh told herself. For the last few weeks, she had been trying to negotiate between her department, the farmers' union, and the company. The potential benefits of the collaboration were so big that it was in nobody's interest to stop the initiative. Yet the farmers were not happy and threatened to walk out.

For Lanh, the ultimate goal was clear: thousands of farmers would get access to irrigated farmland and new technology, and their livelihoods would be more secure against impacts from climate change. Apparently, these benefits were not so obvious to the other stakeholders.

Lanh started to doubt. Was the farmers' reaction due to personalities? Was she the only one trying to bridge this huge divide between stakeholders? Was conflict unavoidable?

a government official

"I am, personally very interested in getting a better understanding of alternative approaches to climate negotiations as one such multi-stakeholder process seeking to establish a new (form of) climate governance. We are currently locked in camps that behave more like a bunch of school kids in the playground than as parties to a really challenging common agenda. A question I constantly ask myself in these circumstances is: to what extent do the current approaches of negotiation contribute to or stand in the way of a true multi-stakeholder process, and how could we create the enabling conditions that would make this process more efficient?"

(Email from a government official engaged in climate change negotiations)

What is conflict?
And what do we mean by 'dealing with' it?

Conflict is what happens when parties disagree with each other on an important issue, and see their different positions as essentially incompatible. It is almost inevitable in any MSP, as different stakeholders will naturally have different interests, and are likely to find it difficult to imagine an acceptable compromise. If you want your MSP to be effective, it is essential that conflict is not ignored or pushed aside but is instead addressed and handled constructively.

There are two main types of conflict in an MSP. The first is where conflict is the key reason for establishing the MSP, for example, conflict between environmental and economic interests with competing claims on how natural resources are used. The second is conflict that emerges when different stakeholders try to work together in an MSP. These may range from conflicts over fundamental issues related to different views, values, and competition for resources, to more simple clashes between personalities or resulting from miscommunication.

Conflict as a reason for an MSP	Conflict emerging within an MSP
Example: The Ruaha river in Tanzania has been drying up for decades. This is a catastrophe for the wildlife in the Ruaha National Park, and impacts the livelihoods of downstream communities and tourism in the park. Conservationists blame intensive agriculture upstream for tapping off too much water. But farmers need irrigation to increase their productivity in order to survive. WWF-Tanzania and WWF-UK took part in a multi-stakeholder partnership initiated so that the different parties could 'learn together to find a way out of the crisis'.	Example: Farmers and agribusiness in an African country were interested in developing stronger linkages to local markets. They started working together supported by an NGO to learn how to make this happen. A secretariat was set up, hosted by the NGO. After a year, the different partners complained that the secretariat was only advancing the interests of the NGO. The mistrust grew, and what started as a genuine effort to collaborate, became a ground for conflict. It took an external mediator six months to normalise relationships.

In the following, we look at three perspectives that will help you recognise and deal with conflict: exploring causes of conflicts, a continuum of conflict, and interest-based negotiation.

Perspective 1: Causes of conflict

Conflicts begin and persist for all sorts of reasons, and their origins are often complex and diverse. They can be embedded in local cultural systems or connected to wider social, economic, and political processes. We find Moore's distinction of different types of conflict useful for recognising and dealing with the different causes:

a) **Data or fact conflicts** (disputes over the validity of information): "...you are grossly overstating the number of land grabs by companies in South Sudan. What do you base these values on?"

b) **Needs or interest conflicts** (competing interests): "...there is not enough water for all of us to do what we need to. It's either for your company or for my farm."

c) **Structural conflicts** (issues related to laws, roles and responsibility, time constraints): "...it is a disgrace that women are still not allowed to fully participate in political decision-making."

d) **Value conflicts** (differing values): "...these people keep telling us that the market will solve everything and create prosperity for all. I can't buy into that, and refuse to work with them on their conditions."

e) **Relationship conflicts** (personality differences): "...why is he always so keen to talk to the press... I think his ego might be too big..."

Conflicts are changing, interactive social processes, rather than individual, self-contained events. And each conflict has its own unique history and its own course of phases and levels of intensity. Essentially, conflicts are about the perceptions and the (different) meanings that people give to events, policies, institutions, and others. Thus, there is no single true or objective account of a conflict. Rather, the participants in and the observers of conflicts are likely to interpret them differently, depending on their particular perspective and interests.

Different underlying causes require different solutions. You may be able to address the causes of conflict in an MSP directly (e.g., by improving and sharing information, building relationships and shared values, and allowing time for different stakeholders to understand each other's interests) or indirectly (e.g., by arriving at a shared understanding of how laws need to change).

Perspective 2: Continuum of conflict

Not all conflicts are the same. They can range in intensity from an irritating difference of opinion to a major disagreement with complete breakdown of communication, and even violent action. Different strategies are needed for dealing with conflicts at different points along the continuum. Some may only be resolved through the legal system; more severe conflicts may result in violence and war. MSPs generally work at the end of the spectrum where there is space for discussion, negotiation, and arbitration, and these are the skills that you will need to develop.

Moore (2014)
Continuum of conflict management and resolution approaches

Private decision making by parties				Private third-party decision making		Legal (public), authoritative third-party decision making		Extralegal coerced decision making	
Conflict avoidance	Informal discussion + problem	Negotiation	Mediation	Administrative decision	Arbitration	Judicial decision	Legislative decision	Nonviolent direct action	Violence

→

Increased coercion and likelihood of win-lose outcome →

Not all those involved in a conflict will view it in the same way. The different parties involved will have their own subjective ideas of the intensity of the conflict, and whether it is escalating or calming down. This also means that they will have different ideas about what is needed to resolve it. Those who think it is escalating may feel that formal authoritative approaches offer the only possibility for resolution, while those who feel that it is lessening may suggest that now is a good time to start talking and negotiating. When conflicts arise in your MSP, you will need to look at each party's perceptions of the stage of the conflict before starting to develop a conflict management, transformation, or resolution strategy.

Moore (2014)
Causes of conflict

RELATIONSHIP CONFLICTS

1. Miscommunication
2. Strong emotions
3. Stereotyping
4. Repetitive negative behaviour

INTEREST CONFLICTS

1. Percieved or actual competition over interests
2. Procedural interests
3. Psychological interests

DATA CONFLICTS

1. lack of information
2. Misinformation
3. Differing views on data's relevance
4. Different interpretations of data

VALUE CONFLICTS

1. Different ways of life (ideology, worldview, ect.)
2. Different criterias for evaluating ideas

STRUCTURAL CONFLICTS

1. Unequal authority
2. Unequal control of resources
3. Time constraints

Perspective 3: Interest-based negotiation

It is almost inevitable that there will be some conflict in your MSP, and it is important that you can help the stakeholders to negotiate effectively on their different interests. It won't always be possible to define a common goal, and negotiating is the best way to make sure that all parties can achieve a deal that they can be proud to take home to their constituencies and colleagues. Done well, negotiation can prevent or resolve conflicts. But many efforts at negotiation remain unsuccessful, usually because they fail to build consensus in the process.

We find that **interest-based negotiation** is often much more effective in developing a good deal than hard bargaining. A good deal means a deal that is (1) clear, (2) acceptable and attractive to all parties, and (3) better than each party's best alternative.

The key point of this method is to look beyond the stated positions of the different parties to discover their real interests.
• **Position** = the first demand or solution presented by someone, often dogmatic and usually not considerate of other points of view
• **Interest** = elements that underpin the stated 'position' (e.g., drivers, priorities, hopes, external pressures), but which are often obscured and hard to detect

In general, negotiating groups will have a number of interests in common,

Conflict resolution and the Gulpener brewery[27]

The Dutch brewery Gulpener wanted to source its barley locally in a sustainable manner, but farmers in the vicinity preferred to grow maize. The nature conservationist NGO Das en Boom also had concerns in the area; the korenwolf (a type of hamster) was on the brink of extinction because its habitat was disappearing. Traditionally, the company, farmers, and conservationists were at loggerheads with each other, but with the Ministry of Agriculture and Nature Conservation acting as a facilitator, they realised that they had a shared interest and could formulate an agreement that would benefit all parties:
• Farmers agreed to replace their maize with barley because the brewery guaranteed that they would buy the crop at a good price.
• Nature conservationists agreed to support the re-introduction of the korenwolf in the area as the animal thrives where barley is grown. The NGO publically endorsed the brewery's corporate social responsibility.

The brewery signed long-term barley sourcing agreements with the farmers, and introduced 'Korenwolf Beer' at a premium price in 1994. Part of the proceeds of beer sales go to the hamster-breeding programme. Twenty years later, this win–win–win programme still exists and there are still hamster in the area. Gulpener brewery was voted 'Best Family-owned Business in the Netherlands' in 2014.

even when their stated positions have no overlap. All negotiations are harder when they are framed in 'zero-sum' or win–lose terms, as happens when you focus on the stated position. Progress or breakthrough comes when you get beneath the position and can understand and address the underlying interests. The shared interests will often open up new grounds for solutions and better deals. Your aim in supporting an MSP is to bring stakeholders to their senses, not to their knees.

Interest-based negotiation has five main ingredients:[26]
1. Demonstrating genuine interest in the individual's position so your questions are warm, not hostile ("help me to understand why you feel this so strongly…")
2. Gathering information from a range of sources to give you insight into the surrounding circumstances and issues
3. Being sensitive to issues of power (real or perceived) and being respectful but – where necessary – firm ("I can see that in your position it must be very difficult to…")
4. Widening the options by exploring a range of new approaches or alternative solutions ("I wonder if there are any other ways we could …?")
5. Reaching agreement that takes the underlying interests into account and adds more value for those involved

See Principle 3: Work with power

Interest-Based Negotiation

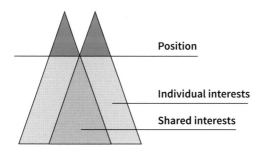

Position

Individual interests

Shared interests

"I once facilitated a transnational workshop for nature conservation in the Balkans. Stakeholders from Serbia, Montenegro, Bosnia and Herzegovina, and Croatia were making plans to manage transboundary nature reserves together. During the meeting, some of the researchers present stressed the need to collect data at these sites. But once the topic of data collection was opened, the language of the meeting changed back from English into Serbian, Bosnian, Montenegrin, and Croatian – similar languages but with differences. The tones of voice changed, facial expressions changed. It transpired that in these transboundary areas, data collection was still largely hindered by landmines – a remnant of the war fought in the nineties. The researchers had unknowingly hit a nerve that exposed a huge underlying unresolved conflict. The atmosphere in the room was grim. From my position at the whiteboard, I moved silently to a chair, sat down, and desperately proposed "Shall we maybe just go for a beer now before moving back to our planning?". "I think we need something stronger!" was the response. Later in the afternoon, we proceeded with the agenda. Of course, we didn't resolve the conflict. But acknowledging that it was still there, and that people's feelings mattered, provided enough space to continue carefully." - Esther Koopmanschap CDI

Practical implications

Considering the following key elements will help you to deal effectively with conflict in your MSP:

Different people respond in different ways to conflict situations. To explore your predominant conflict style, see Section 6: Tool 37

· Understand and work with the underlying causes. The negative relationships may be caused by political, social, or economic structures.

· Understand the behaviours, mental models, and emotions that stakeholders bring to the table. You can't ask other people to change their beliefs. Each person is free to make his or her own choices. But you can create the conditions for people to become aware of their beliefs and the beliefs of others. Through dialogue, we can provide a safe place for people to be honest about their beliefs and to shift their perspectives.

· Don't be too afraid of conflict. We naturally surround ourselves with similar people who confirm what we already think. To change what we think sometimes means surrounding ourselves with people who can be counted upon to prove us wrong. Daring to disagree is an underrated skill.[28]

· Create conversations in your MSP that help people to become less fixed in their positions. You may need to carefully manage the 'emotional hygiene factors' to prevent gossiping, hostility, unwillingness to collaborate, and partisanship. You should also try to craft powerful questions that deepen conversations.

See Principle 5, Perspective 3: Powerful questions

· Identify the possible approaches you could use to deal with the conflict: dialogue (informal or organised), mediation, or interest-based negotiation.

Questions for designing and facilitating MSPs

· Is this conflict caused by the issue on the table, or is it caused by the interaction dynamics of this particular group of stakeholders?

· Are the stakeholders expecting, anticipating, and prepared for conflict?

· Have the scope and limitations of the MSP been recognised in dealing with the conflict?

· What existing mechanisms could be used to deal with the conflict?

· Is the conflict − and how to deal with it − being (openly) discussed?

· Are facilitation processes being used to work through and avoid unnecessary conflict?

PRINCIPLE 5:
Communicate effectively

People being able to communicate with each other in an open, respectful, honest, empathetic, and critical way is one of the key factors underlying an effective MSP. To communicate in this way means being able to listen to others, as well as to be clear when talking about your own perspectives and ideas. Weak communication skills often act as a barrier to multi-stakeholder collaboration. Good communication is the cornerstone of effective collaboration; without it, how can stakeholders overcome their differences and allow new ideas to emerge? The following will help you understand what lies behind effective communication, what is involved in intercultural communication, and how you can develop an effective personal style.

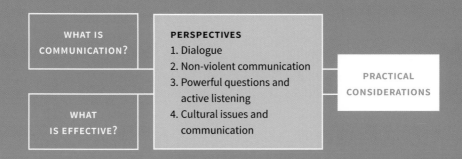

WHAT IS COMMUNICATION?

WHAT IS EFFECTIVE?

PERSPECTIVES
1. Dialogue
2. Non-violent communication
3. Powerful questions and active listening
4. Cultural issues and communication

PRACTICAL CONSIDERATIONS

Paul

It was a great opportunity for Paul of Agri-Inputs Ltd. His boss was out of town, and had texted him last night: "Paul, could you represent our company at the World Bank tomorrow? Stakeholder meeting about climate-smart agriculture at 14:00".

It was Paul's first time at the World Bank office. He decided to listen carefully so that he could report back to his boss. The discussion was complex and the language used was intimidating. Paul didn't dare to say more than his name and function during the introduction round. He was familiar with the topic, and his company had an urgent interest in developing new solutions. Yet he was not sure if it was appropriate for him to speak on behalf of the company.

So Paul kept silent. How could a junior staff member speak to all these important people?

There were follow-up meetings after this one. The World Bank never invited Agri-Inputs Ltd. back. They assumed that the company wasn't interested after they sent a junior who didn't say anything.

What is communication, and what is effective?

We often take communication for granted and don't give it the attention it deserves. But weak basic communication skills can easily limit the potential of an MSP. For an MSP to address issues effectively, the people at the heart of the problem need to work together to develop a shared understanding of the situation and create something new. For this, they need to communicate effectively.

If an MSP is to make a difference, it needs to find ways of getting people to engage with each other's perspectives. The people involved need to suspend judgment and listen to and understand each other's views (even if they don't agree), underlying needs, and assumptions. This means developing effective skills for, and cultures of, communication.

See Principle 1, Perspective 2: Systems thinking with the iceberg

Much has been written about the different factors underlying communication problems. To us, a few key ideas stand out:

1. **Divergent underlying paradigms or views:** each person has a set of beliefs, worldviews, and paradigms about the world he or she lives in. Paradigms are essential for making sense of the world, but they are often so internalised that we aren't aware of them; we then experience misunderstandings when we assume that other people see things in the same way as us.

2. **Judging rather than engaging with others' views:** Because of our different worldviews and different interests, we also tend to evaluate or judge what others are saying, rather than engaging directly with what is being said.

3. **Embedded conversational habits when talking and listening:** Most of us tend to talk without listening, and respond immediately to what someone says without thinking about what it really means.

4. **Emotional responses:** Especially when the communication is about important and sensitive issues, people's emotional response to what is being said can make it difficult to take it in, or to respond in a way that deepens their understanding of what has been said.

5. **Conflict or lack of trust.**

See Principle 4: Deal with conflict

Sometimes communication simply doesn't occur, because people don't trust each other or there is an underlying conflict between them. In the following, we look at four perspectives that will help you to understand how effective communication skills can increase the chances that your MSP will yield results: dialogue, non-violent communication, powerful questions and active listening, and cultural issues and communication. If you are interested in how MSPs communicate with the outside world (general public, constituencies), you will find more in Section 5.

Perspective 1: Dialogue versus debate

Dialogue is a conversation in which people think together in a relationship, suspend their judgment, and together create something new (new social realities). People who are in a dialogue set out to understand the other person's perspective, even if they don't agree with it. They have an open and curious attitude, and the focus is on collective learning and looking for new things. Dialogue is fundamentally different to a debate, in which people try to persuade or convince others of the validity of a particular view.

A good starting point for working towards creating a dialogue is to differentiate the approach from debate. You can use the questions in the table to analyse a conversation and decide whether it is more debate or dialogue. You can also use these questions as a guideline for transforming a debate into a dialogue. At CDI, we sometimes use debates in order to get the issues clear and uncover the underlying paradigms or mindsets. This works particularly well in training or action research settings where issues are explored. But as soon as stakeholders face the task of co-creating something new, you will find it more effective to design a dialogue process.

Dialogue versus Debate	Debate	Dialogue
The premise	Does each speaker consider only one right answer or perspective, normally his/her own?	Do speakers consider many possible right answers and perspectives, including their own?
The goal	Is the goal to win, to be right, to sell the idea, persuade, or convince?	Is the goal to understand the other from his/her perspective? (Understanding doesn't mean agreeing.)
The attitude	Are people being evaluative and critical?	Are people curious and open?
The focus	Is the focus on what is lacking in a particular idea or perspective? Or on the weak points?	Is the focus on what is new? Of value? What you can learn?
The behaviour	Are people talking more than they listen? Are people listening with judgment? Are people asking questions to question the other? Do people see their assumptions as the truth?	Are people listening more than they talk? Are people listening without judgment? Are people asking questions to clarify and understand? Do people see their assumptions as an alternative?

Conversation is a meeting of minds with different memories and habits. When minds meet, they don't just exchange facts: they transform them, reshape them, draw different implications from them, and engage in new trains of thought. Conversation doesn't just reshuffle the cards: it creates new cards. – Theodore Zeldin[29]

The flowchart by William Isaacs[30] shown in the figure can help you to distinguish between different types of conversation. At each stage of an MSP, you should ask the question: "What type of conversation do we need at this point in time?" A dialogue in which stakeholders engage with the deeper questions and assumptions may be ideal to co-create new solutions and insights (generative dialogue). But there are also times when it is essential to discuss hard facts and data in order to establish agreement (dialectic).

If a dialogue is 'a conversation with a centre, not sides', as William Isaacs argues,[31] the question is what should be in this centre. It is not usually a powerful speaker with a PowerPoint presentation. More often, it is a well-crafted question. Generative questions will help a group to think together, instead of having a series of individuals thinking alone in one room. Thinking together implies that you no longer take your own position as final. The art of convening a dialogue is to help participants move beyond their business-as-usual way of competing with ideas.

> You can find some tips on crafting good questions in Perspective 3 Powerful Questions

In Principle 4 (Value Conflict), we discussed negotiation as a technique that is sometimes necessary in order to reach agreement. Dialogue goes further: its intention is to reach a new understanding and, in doing so, to form a completely new basis from which to think and act. In dialogue, you not only solve problems, you dissolve them.

Finally, designing and facilitating a dialogue cannot be learned from a book. Find ways to practice, observe others, and reflect. You can't separate your own personality, emotions, and ideas from convening a dialogue. Section 5 provides further details on how facilitators of MSPs can prepare themselves for these roles.

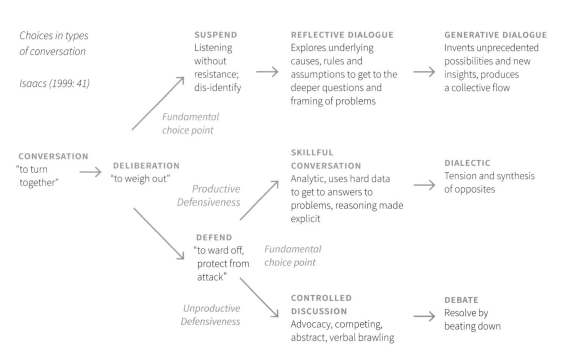

Choices in types of conversation

Isaacs (1999: 41)

SUSPEND
Listening without resistance; dis-identify

Fundamental choice point

REFLECTIVE DIALOGUE
Explores underlying causes, rules and assumptions to get to the deeper questions and framing of problems

GENERATIVE DIALOGUE
Invents unprecedented possibilities and new insights, produces a collective flow

CONVERSATION
"to turn together"

DELIBERATION
"to weigh out"

Productive Defensiveness

SKILLFUL CONVERSATION
Analytic, uses hard data to get to answers to problems, reasoning made explicit

DIALECTIC
Tension and synthesis of opposites

DEFEND
"to ward off, protect from attack"

Fundamental choice point

Unproductive Defensiveness

CONTROLLED DISCUSSION
Advocacy, competing, abstract, verbal brawling

DEBATE
Resolve by beating down

Perspective 2: Non-violent communication

The idea of non-violent communication or NVC was developed by Marshall
Rosenberg in the late 1960s during his involvement with racial integration in
the Southern United States. He was fascinated by two fundamental questions:
1. If humans like to support each other and care for each other, why do we
   create so much violence and suffering through our interactions, even
   towards those we love?
2. Equally, how are some people able to stay compassionate, even under the
   most difficult and violent circumstances?

Rosenberg became convinced that part of the answer to these questions
could be found in the way people communicate. His methodology is applied
worldwide, supported by his Center for Non-Violent Communication,[32] and
is also used in professional settings, where it focuses on communication that
connects.

How we communicate greatly influences the quality of our work relationships.
We can find it very rewarding if we are able to exchange our inner thoughts
with colleagues and stakeholders. But often our way of communicating
doesn't help us reach that level of contact. We say things like "That's just
the way I am, I can't change that", or "Haven't you finished that report yet?
You're always late!". Remarks like these only leave you with the choice of
fighting or fleeing.

Rosenberg developed an alternative way of communicating. Non-violent
communication encourages us to focus on what we and others observe,
how we feel about it, what our underlying needs are, and what each of us
would request from others, or from ourselves. It acknowledges feelings and
emphasises talking about and connecting with the needs, and offers a chance
to connect with yourself as well as others. Connecting with yourself results in
more clarity and offers an opening for compassion, and for moving forward in
new ways. This means that practicing non-violent communication can help
to prevent escalation, and can help you to get things done effectively without
violating other people's interests.

Can non-violent communication be useful in an MSP setting? In our
experience, many participants in MSPs have only a limited awareness of
their style of communication, and of the deeper drivers that influence the
way in which we interact with others. Increasing this awareness can help
stakeholders to become more perceptive and to listen to the needs of others,
and can help them to express their own needs more effectively too.

*People have been trained to criticise, insult, and
otherwise communicate in ways that create distance
among people. – Marshall Rosenberg[33]*

Non-violent communication has four components:

Observation - The concrete actions we are **observing** that are affecting our wellbeing
Feeling - How we are **feeling** in relation to what we are observing
Needs - The **needs**, values, desires, and so on that are creating our feelings
Request - The concrete actions we **request** in order to enrich our lives

Essentially, in NVC you reflect on your own way of communicating using 'I' (or you) statements for the four components. You do this both for your role of listening empathetically and for your role of expressing honestly.

Empathetic listening	Expressing honestly
Observations ("When you see…")	Observations ("When I see…")
Feelings ("…are you feeling…")	Feelings ("… I feel…")
Needs ("…because you need…")	Needs ("…because I need…")
Requests ("Would you like me to…")	Requests ("Would you be willing to…")

We can use the situation of Paul at the beginning of this section as an example. He kept silent during the World Bank meeting. Now what might the World Bank facilitator say to Paul if they met again:

Observation: "Weren't you interested in the meeting? You were silent all the time!" **Feeling:** "I felt I wasn't being taken seriously as a facilitator…" **Need:** "…and I needed you to speak out and share". **Request:** "I want you to participate actively next time"

You can imagine that this message might set Paul on the defensive, and it might not help the facilitator to connect to what is going on inside Paul, or to get the desired result. Now let's consider another way in which the facilitator could respond using non-violent communication:

Observation: "The meeting went on for an hour and a half and you said only a few words at the beginning of the meeting, keeping silent for the rest of the time." **Feeling:** "I felt insecure, but also frustrated and annoyed…" **Need:** "…because I wanted to be reassured that you were at ease in my meeting" **Request:** "What can I do to make you feel comfortable enough to share your opinion next time?"

The benefit of using non-violent communication is that you can become more articulate in expressing yourself, and more empathetic in listening. You need to use words that refer to specifics: specific observations, specific needs, specific feelings, and specific requests. And use 'I' statements: I see this, I have this need, I feel this way, I request. This can help you and your stakeholders to avoid falling into the trap of making aggressive statements (judging others, express quasi-feelings, making demands on others) which do not help the group to think collectively.

Perspective 3: Powerful questions and active listening

When you want to stimulate communication among stakeholders, you need to craft good questions to frame the conversation. This was one of the points discussed in Perspective 1: Dialogue versus Debate. You can employ as many participatory tools as you want; if there is no appropriate question or invitation, your stakeholder process will not yield results. In the following, we explore what makes a question powerful, and what makes a good listener.

See Section 3, Process model

First, you will need to decide what type of conversation you want to have with your stakeholders. This depends on the phase of your collaboration, as well as the level of goal clarity, analytical clarity, and trust and consensus in the group. In general, open questions ("Why are we here?") are more powerful than closed questions ("Can we agree on the current proposal or not?"), as open questions invite new thinking and have the capacity to move a system towards innovation.

There are three types of powerful questions:
(1) Questions for focusing collective attention (e.g., "What's important to you about climate change in Ethiopia and why do you care?")
(2) Questions for connecting ideas and finding deeper insight (e.g., "What's been your/our major learning, insight, or discovery so far?")
(3) Questions that create forward movement (e.g., "What's possible here and who cares?" rather than "What's wrong here and who's responsible?").

Play around with crafting questions that will work in your context. Remember that good questions don't always need to be answered fully. They should enable a different, better conversation. Finally, what makes a good listener? At CDI, we find that good stakeholder meetings are not only about lively dialogue and the exchange of views and ideas, but also about a certain quality of listening. Such listening is needed to ensure that any suggestions are taken

According to Vogt, Brown, and Isaacs,[34]

A powerful question:	**Check yourself**
• generates curiosity in the listener	You know you're not listening when:
• stimulates reflective conversation	• You're finishing other peoples' sentences
• is thought-provoking	• Trigger words send your thoughts wandering
• surfaces underlying assumptions	• You're focusing on vocabulary or a way of speaking
• invites creativity and new possibilities	• You're thinking about what you're going to say next
• generates energy and forward movement	
• channels attention and focuses inquiry	
• stays with stakeholders	• You feel that your attention span is limited
• touches a deep meaning	• You're thinking about how you feel about what was just said
• evokes more questions	

seriously, to connect ideas that are shared, and to build trust. In any act of communication, we need to realise that our assumptions, stereotypes, and expectations filter and colour the way we perceive messages.

Active listening means clearing your mind as much as possible and being fully attentive to the other person – without judgement, prejudice, or foregone conclusions. It requires the listener to feed back what they hear to the speaker, by way of re-stating or paraphrasing what they have heard in their own words, to confirm what they have heard, and to confirm the understanding of both parties. Some people are naturally better than others at listening actively. But like non-violent communication, active listening is a skill that can be learned. Remember to design processes in such a way that the contribution of the quiet listeners is also taken into account.[35]

See
Perspective 2

I hope he doesn't find out that I just started this job and hardly know the jargon.

I actually like him, but my colleagues think he's the enemy.

If he is from an NGO he's probably going to leak to the press - so I'd better be careful.

**Assumptions
Stereotypes
Expectations**

I have no expectations from this meeting. The previous ones were all manipulated by the company.

NGOs are all the same. You give them an inch and they'll take a mile.

I am completely exhausted after a night flight and running 3 jobs to make ends meet.

*Many things
influence the
way we see,
listen and assess
others, and
ourselves, in
interaction*

Appoint a listening scout

*"We were concerned that some agenda topics at our
conference wouldn't get the attention they deserved.
So we appointed 'scouts' for each topic, who would
listen to and observe that particular topic on top of
their normal conference participation. On the final
day, we asked them to give a plenary 'scout reflection',
which was insightful for everybody. The scouts also
remarked that the listening assignment had helped
them to participate more effectively" - Wijnand van
IJssel, Dutch Ministry of Foreign Affairs.*

*Field staff versus coordinators – and
the role of outsiders*

*"We support agricultural innovation in
Ethiopia. There are many farmer-led
experiments going on at the district
level. It is usually the local and junior
staff who know most about what
is actually going on at field level.
But at formal meetings, junior staff
often don't speak openly about these
experiences. It is culturally important
in Ethiopia to listen to those who are in
charge and avoid contradicting your
boss.*

*Being a young international
consultant, I try to give these
knowledgeable local staff a voice by
travelling with them to the field. In the
car, I often ask informal questions to
make them feel at ease and they tell
me their stories – also the things they
find difficult to say to their bosses.
Often I am able – as an outsider – to
bring this information back into policy
discussions with the senior managers.
This does not embarrass anybody,
and in fact some managers now give
me questions 'to discuss in the car' if
they want to know the real situation.
So even when culture prevents open
communication, there are ways to
improve the flow of information."*

Perspective 4: Cultural issues in communication

We all know that different cultures have different patterns and styles of communication. And the same is true of the participants in MSPs, who are likely to come from different sectors, different age groups, different organisations, and even different countries, each with its own way of communicating. Business culture is very different to the culture found in civil society and government; communication in grassroots groups can be very different to that in a big INGO or multinational company. Good communication in mixed settings doesn't just happen by itself; it needs to be fostered and encouraged by increasing awareness and understanding.

The success of an MSP depends to some extent on the ability of the stakeholders to choose ways of interacting that respect the cultural preferences of the other participants. Not everybody finds efficient business meetings pleasant (most public sector and NGO workers and academics prefer longer in-depth exchanges). Nor will everyone be happy to speak their mind in a meeting with strangers (most Asian and African professionals prefer to have clear mandates from their superiors).

So is it possible to satisfy everybody? Probably not. In our experience, however, there are some things that can be done to ease communication between cultures:

- The first rule of thumb is to know who is in the room. Familiarise yourself with the backgrounds of the different stakeholders: their nationality, corporate culture, preferences for interacting interpersonally and in larger groups, and how they would like to be addressed.
- Second, look at the meeting design and assess whether everybody will feel comfortable enough to communicate openly. If not, try to make variations in the programme. For example, in a participatory workshop include a formal keynote speech by a high-ranking official in order to pay respect to more hierarchical cultural practices. Or if the programme is already quite formal, include buzz sessions where groups of 2–3 people talk together for 10 minutes to allow for more sharing of ideas, which is appreciated by people with a cultural background in which exchange and brainstorming are the norm.
- Third, grasp every opportunity to create a common language among stakeholders. This can be through the introduction of new terminology (which is not associated with one party in particular), but most of all it should be through encounters. Joint exposure visits, extended introduction exercises, and informal dinners can all help to increase the connections and ease communication among stakeholders.
- Finally, have a special bias towards stakeholders who you suspect to be culturally not at ease in this stakeholder meeting. Some voices need to be amplified to be heard. This is not choosing sides for one party over another; it is being a good facilitator. If participants feel insecure, for example because they have less formal education, try to ensure that somebody is present to coach them prior to and during the meeting. You can also help with some capacity building activities before they engage with the other stakeholders.

See Principle 3, Work with power

Practical implications

Look at the five main factors underlying communication problems and consider whether and how they could be an issue in your MSP. This will give you a good framework for developing a strategy to ensure that communication in your MSP is constructive, and that failure in communication doesn't hinder progress.

· Ensure that time is invested at the start in understanding the different views of the problem and their underlying paradigms. In the initiating phase of an MSP, people often assume that all stakeholders understand the problem or issue in the same way. But the problem may be seen rather differently by ordinary citizens, NGOs, government, academia, and the private sector. People are tempted to move too quickly to talking about solutions and possible strategies.

· Use debate to uncover underlying assumptions, for example about the interests of the private sector, as these hamper open communication. Stakeholders often compete about who has the 'right' answer to the problem. To avoid this, make sure that participants get to know and use each other's ideas and strengths.

· Identify, understand, and create awareness about communication patterns, and help your stakeholders to become active listeners and break bad habits. Our active listening skills are often weak due to the way we have been raised and educated. Most of us tend to talk without listening and respond immediately to what someone says, rather than listening and suspending judgement.

· Help your participants to recognise and acknowledge their emotions and those of others, and to understand their sources, before starting the dialogue. Emotional responses also influence the way we communicate. It can be very difficult to listen properly when your emotions are raised.

· Try to build trust and resolve conflicts through open communication and increasing understanding of the different points of view. Lack of trust and conflict can interfere with communication. It isn't easy to share responsibilities when people don't trust each other.

Questions for designing and facilitating MSPs

· Are the blockages in an MSP communication related? Are participants (with the facilitator) aware of when communication is going wrong? Are they aware of the communication patterns? Is there a need to improve people's communication competence?

· Do people come from different backgrounds with different worldviews? Has sufficient time been taken to create a shared language and understanding?

· Is the facilitation process helping to support and develop effective communication?

· Have trust and motivation been built? Are emotions being acknowledged and their sources understood? Have underlying needs and assumptions been surfaced?

PRINCIPLE 6:
Promote collaborative leadership

Leadership patterns and capacities can have a profound influence on the direction of an MSP. You may have personal experience of working in a group that performed as a team, and remember feeling very committed. Or you may remember a very formal type of leadership that was clear, but also made you feel a little fearful. To be successful, MSPs need to have a strong collaborative leadership pattern. The people who take on formal and informal leadership roles need to support and promote the collaborative principles that form the basis of the MSP. The following will give you some ideas for developing a good style in both formal and informal leadership roles.

"Leadership is an action that everyone can take. Not a position that a few people can hold." - Paul Schmitz, Collective Impact Forum

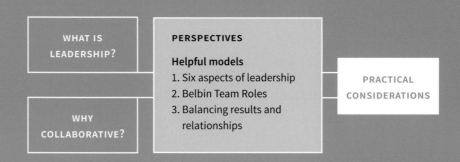

WHAT IS LEADERSHIP?

WHY COLLABORATIVE?

PERSPECTIVES

Helpful models
1. Six aspects of leadership
2. Belbin Team Roles
3. Balancing results and relationships

PRACTICAL CONSIDERATIONS

Sonya

It had started beautifully: good intentions were expressed by everyone, and an MoU was drawn up and signed. This created a nice photo opportunity, which was quickly shared on Twitter and Facebook. On the wings of all this new energy, Sonya had given her very best to coordinate the stakeholder task force.

Yet after some time, when the novelty had worn off, the initiative became routine. Sonya kept going but more and more people seemed to take a backseat, and just tagged along without doing much.

"Of course I understand that I do most of the work, as the appointed coordinator of the task force" Sonya confided to her colleague Jose. "But is it too much to expect others to also do something? It is our joint work plan after all, isn't it?" Jose looked at the ceiling. "I guess you're right Sonya. But the real milestone is not the photo opportunity – it's when everybody knows what to do and is doing it. It sounds like you need a strategy for that..."

What is leadership? And why collaborative?

Behind any successful MSP, you will find effective leadership. We are not talking here about a single dominant leader or a master facilitator. MSPs are all about enabling people to work together, to take responsibility, and to become empowered to tackle difficult issues. This means that an MSP requires collaborative leadership with a range of players taking on various leadership roles – enabling and inspiring leadership styles are critical. We use the term 'collaborative leadership' to refer both to sharing leadership responsibilities and to the particular styles of leadership that are likely to be most effective.

One commonly held fallacy about MSPs is the role that facilitators play. Certainly skilled facilitators can make a great contribution, but in the end, success will largely be determined by how the leaders of the different stakeholder groups take up leadership roles within the stakeholder partnership. MSPs mostly bring different groups together on a voluntary basis, so it is important to understand that leadership approaches that work in a hierarchical setting where leaders have formal authority probably won't work in this more collaborative environment.

In the following, we look at three perspectives that will help you to grasp the idea of collaborative leadership: six aspects of leadership, the Belbin team roles, and balancing power and love.

Perspective 1: Six aspects of leadership in an MSP

Our work suggests that an MSP needs the following six types or areas of leadership.

Convening leadership: These are people who are able to articulate and frame the issues in ways that motivate stakeholders to come together. They are generally respected and trusted figures who are able to build relationships across different stakeholder groups.

Constituency leadership: MSPs can fail when a particular stakeholder group (constituency) does not feel well represented, or is uninformed or under-informed. Leaders of stakeholder groups need to actively engage with their constituency and genuinely represent the group's interests. They need to be able both to help their constituency and to understand the interests of the other groups. MSP activities can never involve everyone, so this bridging between what is happening in the multi-stakeholder space and the individual stakeholder groups is a key leadership function.

Supporting leadership: MSPs will often need support and acceptance from powerful people who may not be directly involved – for example, a government minister or the CEO of a participating organisation. Having these external leaders understand what is happening and be supportive of the process can be critical in many different ways. One dimension of this is funding: people in leadership positions that lie outside the direct process will often be needed to help make the necessary resources available.

Organising leadership: A successful MSP will have a large amount of organisation behind the scenes. This includes arranging events, organising field visits, mobilising resources, setting up websites, setting up meetings, and many others. An MSP can quickly collapse if this is not done well and stakeholders see the process as disorganised.

Informing leadership: An MSP should be based on stakeholders having access to and using good information about the issues they are concerned with. Leadership is needed to identify what information is needed and to ensure that it is gathered and communicated in ways that the stakeholders can understand and relate to. It is important that this leadership is seen to be working in the interests of all stakeholders, rather than biased in terms of what information is gathered and how it is used.

Facilitation leadership: We know that the effective use of participatory methods and tools dramatically improves collective learning between stakeholders, and thus the effectiveness of the overall process. Leadership is needed to open up space for the use of facilitation methods. And the facilitation itself is an important form of leadership.

If you are initiating an MSP or trying to understand why it may be struggling, ask questions about these different aspects of leadership and how they could be improved. This can help to keep the process on track.

Curious about your own preferred team roles? Section 6, Tool 35 leads to background on Belbin and a self-test.

Functional Role	Team Role
The job we have been hired to do, based upon our ability, experience and skill	Our tendency to behave, contribute and interrelate in certain ways
What we do...	And how we do it...

Perspective 2: Leadership and Belbin Team Roles[36]

Collaborative leadership becomes easier when the team is diverse and stakeholders are aware of the assets they possess together. Dr Meredith Belbin studied teamwork for many years, and observed that people in teams tend to assume different team roles. He defined a team role as "a tendency to behave, contribute, and interrelate with others in a particular way", and described nine different roles that underlie team success.

Belbin suggests that, by understanding your role within a particular team, you can develop your strengths and manage your weaknesses as a team member, and so improve how you contribute to the team. Team leaders and team development practitioners often use the Belbin model to help create more balanced teams. Teams can become unbalanced if all team members have similar styles of behaviour or team roles. If team members have a similar weakness, the team as a whole tends to have that weakness. If team members have similar teamwork strengths, they may tend to compete (rather than co-operate) for the team tasks and responsibilities that best suit their natural styles. Knowing this, you can use the model with your team to help ensure that the necessary team roles are covered, and to address potential behavioural tensions or weaknesses among the team members.[37]

Belbin Team Roles

When we work in a team, each of us will make our most effective contribution when we focus on just two or three of these roles. And an effective team will have members that cover all nine roles.

Team role	Strengths	Allowable weaknesses
Coordinator	Mature, confident, a good chairperson; clarifies goals, promotes decision-making, and delegates well	Can be seen as manipulative; offloads personal work
Teamworker	Co-operative, mild, perceptive, and diplomatic; listens, builds, and averts friction	Indecisive in crunch situations
Resource investigator	Extrovert, enthusiastic, communicative; explores opportunities and delivers contacts	Over-optimistic; loses interest once initial enthusiasm has passed
Plant	Creative, imaginative, unorthodox; solves difficult problems	Ignores details; too preoccupied to communicate effectively
Monitor, evaluator	Sober, strategic, discerning; sees all options and judges accurately	Lacks drive or the ability to inspire others
Specialist	Single-minded, self-starter, dedicated; brings knowledge and skills in rare supply	Contributes only on a narrow front; dwells on technicalities
Shaper	Challenging, dynamic, thrives on pressure; driven to overcoming obstacles	Prone to provocation, offends others' feelings
Implementer	Disciplined, reliable, conservative, efficient; turns ideas into practical action	Somewhat inflexible; slow to respond to new possibilities
Completer, finisher	Painstaking, conscientious, anxious; searches out errors and omissions; delivers on time	Inclined to worry unduly; reluctant to delegate

Perspective 3: Balancing results and relationships

This perspective draws on insights from Adam Kahane, who reflected[38] on his long experience in facilitating MSPs by wondering why things so often went wrong. He asked, "Why do some groups of people manage to solve complex problems, while others stumble or fall?" and came to surprising insights that are relevant for understanding how collaborative leadership can work. Kahane noticed two basic approaches used for solving complex problems in MSPs:

1. Relying on violence and aggression
2. Submitting to endless negotiation and compromise

These two seem difficult to combine, and in reality it's usually either/or. This is because the drives behind these approaches are directly opposed: there is power, the desire to achieve one's purpose, and love, the urge to unite with others. Kahane draws these definitions of power and love from the theologian Paul Tillich[39] Put simply, power equals results-orientation; love equals relationship-orientation. The most successful examples of MSPs have both, and see power and love as complementary.

It isn't easy to gain insight into where your MSP may need a better balance between power and love. You will first need to carry out a rigorous self-assessment. Most people have a natural preference for a power or love approach. If you find that the leadership in your MSP lacks 'power' or 'love' people, then it might be time to restore the balance.

We find this perspective very helpful, because it moves away from the often-heard notion that MSPs are only about developing relationships and collaborative patterns. MSPs are also about getting things done, and are arenas of power play where those with the most force will obtain the best results. Good leadership is not about eliminating power issues – it is about making them work for sustainable results for everybody.

"Power without love is reckless and abusive, and love without power is sentimental and anaemic" - Martin Luther King

An example of balancing power and love

CDI supported a Dutch development NGO that was bringing all its partners together to jointly advocate for better basic health services in rural areas in an African country. The NGO was patient. It did not want to be seen as a dictating top-down donor and chose to follow a lengthy process of participatory consultation to keep everybody on board. Two years of workshops and consultations led to a widely owned context analysis and an outline strategy – but still no results on the ground. Some of the stakeholders grew impatient and threatened to drop out of the collaboration because 'it was going nowhere'. The NGO realised it had applied too much 'love' in its approach to partnering, to the detriment of 'power'. The NGO shifted gear and began to push for results and action on the ground. This upset another group of stakeholders who felt that the atmosphere was changing, resulting in loss of trust and even competition among partners. It took the NGO several years to strike the right balance between power and love, between empathy and resolve. They did so by creating a leadership team that included both results-oriented and relationship-oriented leaders, who agreed to steer and monitor where the partnership was going.

"The deep changes needed to accelerate progress against society's most intractable problems require a unique type of leader – the system leader; a person who catalyses collective leadership." - Peter Senge/Hal Hamilton/John Kania; Stanford Social Innovation Review 2015 .[40]

Practical implications

· Recognise the multiple aspects of leadership that will be critical to the success of your MSP; assess where the leadership strengths and weaknesses lie and look at ways to foster collaborative leadership.

· Be careful to make sure that the facilitators or facilitating organisations don't dominate the leadership functions of the MSP, as this would undermine stakeholder commitment and engagement.

· Help to create effective leadership practices within the constituency groups to ensure that there is good communication, understanding, and representation.

· Take time in the core work of the MSP to strengthen leadership capabilities.

· Support leaders and representatives of stakeholder groups who may be more used to authoritative leadership to adjust to what will work best in an MSP setting.

· Recognise and support the development of the different team roles that underlie collaborative leadership.

Questions for designing and facilitating MSPs

· Even if you have all stakeholders represented, what more can you do to create a sense of collaborative leadership?

· Could your enthusiasm and commitment to the MSP make it difficult for others to feel responsible too?

· What can the MSP do to strengthen the leadership capabilities of weaker stakeholder groups – even if you don't agree with them?

· Different times in the MSPs life cycle can demand different leadership styles in your team. What is currently needed most? What is lacking?

PRINCIPLE 7:
Foster participatory learning

Ask yourself this:
"How do I create learning processes which help
  people go one level deeper?"
"What is needed to make my MSP rationally,
  emotionally, and creatively engaging?"

You could think of an MSP as a play – or a
battleground – for dealing with strategic challenges.
The stakeholders need to learn from the challenges.
Participatory learning happens when adults learn
from each other's experiences in order to solve
problems and innovate. MSPs need to be spaces
where learning can flourish – otherwise they are
missing the point. The following will give you some
insights into how learning can be supported in MSPs.

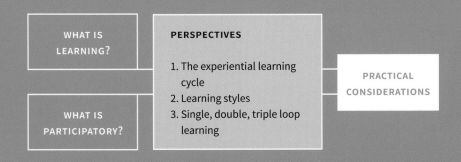

WHAT IS
LEARNING?

WHAT IS
PARTICIPATORY?

PERSPECTIVES

1. The experiential learning
   cycle
2. Learning styles
3. Single, double, triple loop
   learning

PRACTICAL
CONSIDERATIONS

Mahmood

It was 16:30. The first stakeholder meeting had almost ended, and Mahmood became concerned. His agenda topic, 'To develop a culture of excellence through learning' had been squeezed into the meeting agenda at the last moment, and it looked as though the chair would give him exactly three minutes to cover it.

"OK, Mahmood, let's keep going – you wanted to discuss learning. The floor is yours", said the chair. Mahmood delivered his pitch about the need for the partnership to invest in activities that helped them reflect on what they were doing, and identify points for improvement so that the performance of the partnership would be even better.

After his pitch, several participants stared at their watches. Somebody said: "Yeah, interesting idea... can't we just reserve a couple of thousand dollars to send folks for a course? Just to motivate the junior staff. Much easier, too".

Mahmood took a deep breath.

What is participatory learning?

Participatory learning lies at the very heart of any MSP. It is the process that enables different stakeholders to understand each other, to explore common concerns and ambitions, to generate new ideas, and to take joint action. Events and activities are needed throughout the lifetime of an MSP to bring stakeholders together to talk, share, analyse, make decisions, and reflect. The quality of these learning events can make the difference between a successful and a failed MSP.

Let's look more closely at what we mean by learning. Our everyday image of learning is often the 'talk and chalk' model from school. But participatory learning is something very different – it is a process in which adults learn from their own experience in order to solve problems and create improvements. The reason for creating an MSP in the first place is usually that people are 'stuck'. They are facing conflicts, problems, or missed opportunities because the old ways of thinking and acting no longer work, and new ways have not yet been created. The learning process is what makes change possible.

But change is often not easy, and learning is not just about information and knowledge – it is also about our emotions and identities. We feel comfortable in our old patterns of behaviour; admitting that our old prejudices and assumptions no longer make sense can be difficult. Doing new things can feel uncomfortable, even embarrassing. So effective learning processes need to pay attention to the rational, emotional, and creative sides of how our brains function.

An effective MSP needs to create joint learning experiences for the stakeholders in which they feel safe, understood, inspired, and motivated; while at the same time raising critical questions, challenging old assumptions, and using new ideas and information for innovation. This level of engagement is only possible when there is active participation.

In the following, we look at three perspectives that will help you to ensure that participatory and practical learning is woven into the design of your MSP: Kolb's experiential learning cycle; learning styles; and single, double, and triple loop learning.

"Experts can often make valuable contributions, but what is really important is the exploration, thinking, and analysis done by the stakeholders themselves".

Perspective 1: The experiential learning cycle

Much modern thinking about learning in organisations and groups has its roots in the model of experiential learning developed by David Kolb (1984). The experiential learning cycle provides a model of how individuals, groups, or organisations can improve what they are doing by reflecting on their experience. The model shifts the focus of learning from instruction (telling people) to self-reflection and analysis. It offers a very valuable guide for designing learning activities within MSPs, facilitated workshops, and creative learning events.

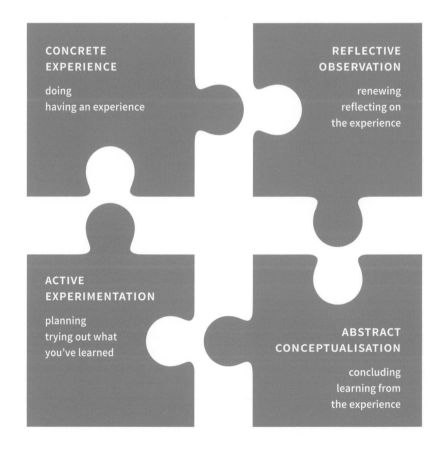

CONCRETE EXPERIENCE

doing
having an experience

REFLECTIVE OBSERVATION

renewing
reflecting on
the experience

ACTIVE EXPERIMENTATION

planning
trying out what
you've learned

ABSTRACT CONCEPTUALISATION

concluding
learning from
the experience

The experiential learning cycle describes learning as a four-stage cyclical process. Individuals or groups must engage in each stage of the cycle in order to learn effectively from their experience and improve the effectiveness of their future actions. The cycle starts with an individual or group experiencing events (or things) – the first stage. This is followed by reflection on the experience – which means exploring what happened, noting your observations, and paying attention to your feelings and those of others. Essentially, you are building up a multidimensional picture of the experience. The third stage involves analysing the information and developing theories, models, or concepts that explain the experience in terms of why things happened the way they did. This theorising or conceptualising is an important part of learning, as it provides the basis for developing solutions to problems using innovative ideas and lateral thinking. It is crucial to draw on existing theories and knowledge, as well as to develop new ideas. Armed with this understanding of past experience, the final stage involves deciding what is most important and trying it out, which means prototyping and testing new ideas. The successful ideas are then put into practice by taking action, which provides a new experience – and the cycle repeats.

See Principle
1, Perspective
3: Adaptive
Management

*Experiential
learning cycle,
based on Kolb
(1984)*

Concrete
experience
feeling

ACTIVIST
Accommodating
Feel and do

REFLECTOR
Diverging
Feel and watch

Active
experimenting
doing

Reflective
observation
watching

PRAGMATIST
Converging
Think and do

THEORIST
Assimilating
Think and watch

Abstract
conceptualization
thinking

Perspective 2: Learning styles

We have found that being explicit about moving through each stage of the learning cycle is a very helpful tool in problem solving, project management, and process facilitation. Different stakeholders tend to have different styles of learning and place more emphasis on, or feel more comfortable at, different stages of the learning cycle. A learning style test[41] based on Kolb's work can help you to determine your own preferred learning style. The box describes the four main archetypal styles.

The four different types of learning style can be plotted on Kolb's cycle as shown below. Some people just like exploring lots of new ideas and situations without moving on to take action ('Reflectors' or 'Theorists'). Some are happy as long as they are busy, and pay less attention to whether what they are doing will produce results ('Pragmatists'). And others tend to jump into action without fully exploring or analysing the whole situation ('Activists'). Being aware of these styles in individuals or groups can dramatically improve problem solving and decision making.

When designing an MSP, you need to make sure that the team represents a good mix of learning styles. We often see great ideas for MSPs being created and promoted by reflectors and theorists, but momentum and credibility is usually created by the actions and follow-through of pragmatists and activists.

Characteristics of different learning styles

You don't only need to have robust learning practices in place to help weaker stakeholders build their capacity. Good learning practices are essential for clarifying the strategy of the MSP and supporting innovation.

Learning style	Description
Activist	Activists learn by doing. They need to get their hands dirty, to dive in feet first. They have an open-minded approach to learning, and involve themselves fully and without bias in new experiences.
Pragmatist	Pragmatists need to be able to see how to put the learning into practice in the real world. They only find abstract concepts and games to be useful when they can see a way to put the ideas into action in their own lives. They are experimenters, trying out new ideas, theories, and techniques to see if they work.
Reflector	Reflectors learn by observing and thinking about what happened. They may avoid leaping in, and prefer to watch from the sidelines. They tend to stand back and view experiences from a number of different perspectives while collecting data; they take time to work towards an appropriate conclusion.
Theorist	Theorists like to understand the theory behind the actions. They need models, concepts, and facts in order to engage in the learning process. They prefer to analyse and synthesise, drawing new information into a systematic and logical theory.

Tip: In meetings with your stakeholders, make a habit of doing a quick round at the end using the question: "Can you give us a main insight from the meeting that you'd like to share with everyone?"

Perspective 3: Single, double, and triple loop learning

Another approach that can help us be more specific about what we learn is to distinguish between single, double, and triple loop learning. These three levels of learning are based on the work of Argyris and Schon.[42]

Single loop learning mainly considers small changes made to practices or behaviours based on what has or has not worked in the past. The approach involves doing things better without necessarily examining or challenging our underlying beliefs and assumptions. Single loop learning leads to minor fixes or adjustments.

Are we doing things right? Here's what to do – procedures or rules.

Double loop learning leads to insights about why a solution works. In this level of process analysis, people become observers of themselves, and ask, "What is going on? What are the patterns?" Understanding the patterns, helps us to change the way we make decisions and deepens our understanding of our assumptions. Double loop learning leads to major fixes or changes, like redesigning an organisational function or structure.

Are we doing the right things? Here's why this works – insights and patterns.

Based on Argyris and Schön (1974)

Triple loop learning involves principles. The learning goes beyond insights and patterns and creates a shift in understanding the context or our point of view. We produce new commitments and ways of learning – we learn how to learn. This learning helps to enhance the way we comprehend the situation and helps

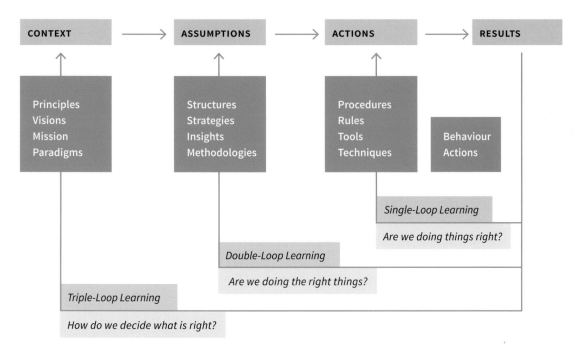

us change our purpose. We develop a better understanding of how to respond to our environment, and deepen our comprehension of why we choose to do the things we do. Triple loop learning is essential for working with MSPs, as the different worldviews and behaviours of multiple stakeholders need to be recognised, understood, and taken into account when choosing how to move forward.

How do we decide what is right? Here's why we want to be doing this – principles.

<table>
<tr>
<td style="border: 1px solid #000;">See Section 7, the story of prof. Ken Giller on how to build learning into your MSP</td>
<td>In MSPs, collaborative action can only take place when stakeholders are committed to questioning their assumptions and the context in which they operate. Effective learning methodologies can help you go beyond superficial learning to double and triple loop learning. Effective learning will alternate between the three types. We cannot always be questioning basic assumptions because if we do, we won't be able to move forward. But if we don't ask deeper questions from time to time, we may move fast but not in the right direction. This means that most learning will be single loop, adjusting what we are doing, but from time to time you will need to take stock of the situation and move to double loop and triple loop learning.</td>
</tr>
</table>

Fortunately, a vast array of participatory methods and tools have been created and tested over the past few decades that can help you to reflect more deeply. Open space, future search, soft systems methodology, world café, rich pictures, mind mapping, and card clustering are just some examples. You can find more details of some of these tools in Section 6, and the Resource section will help you find good books and web-based resources that provide guidance on setting-up and facilitating good learning processes. [43]

Learning loops in practice

A producer organisation in West Africa was trying to improve their market access project, which aimed to link small-scale farmers to international markets. Initially they discussed information gaps in their M&E system. But after having conversations with their stakeholders (small and medium enterprises or SMEs), researchers, government agencies, and NGOs), they realised that the problem wasn't information gaps. Rather, they discovered that several key assumptions in the project were false: the farmers could never meet the quality and quantity requirements of the international market. So they decided to restrategise and focus on local markets, with value addition through processing of the product.

What started as an exercise in single loop learning (improving the M&E system) resulted in deeper questions about strategy (double loop learning). The producer organisation then decided to continue working more closely with the stakeholders to ensure that they would have better access to market intelligence (triple loop learning).

Practical implications

How do you foster good learning processes?

· Create learning environments that are safe... but challenging enough to encourage people to think outside the box and be creative.

· Make learning participatory: it's not something you do to people, but which people do themselves.

· Design MSPs around the experiential learning cycle. This means first exploring the situation without judgment, then analysing the implications from different stakeholder perspectives, then making decisions, and finally taking action. Jumping too early to decisions and action will undermine the learning process.

· Make sure that teams of stakeholders represent different learning styles so that they can benefit from the experiential learning cycle: activists, reflectors, theorists, and pragmatists.

· Choose methods that facilitate single, double, and triple loop learning.

· Remember that learning is not necessarily about building capacity. It's also about innovation: understanding the challenge, identifying new options, and testing until something works.

· Finally, let's be honest: nobody reads standard workshop reports. Extend the principle of fostering participatory learning to the documentation: draw your stakeholders in. Use creative methods: social media, visual harvesting, and so on.

Questions for designing and facilitating MSPs

· Have you thought about what constitutes a good learning climate for your particular group of stakeholders?

· What (creative) methods of documentation will be most effective for capturing the learning?

· What mechanisms are in place to allow the lessons learned to feed back into your MSP's strategy and procedures?

"I am always amazed at what can arise from a collective learning process" – Arie de Geus (pioneer of organizational learning; former Corporate Planning Director of Royal Dutch Shell)

"Tell me, and I will forget. Show me, and I may remember. Involve me, and I will understand" – Confucius around 450 BC

5 FROM DESIGN TO PRACTICE

How can multi-stakeholder partnerships be initiated and facilitated?

Now that you have thought about the process to use in your MSP, and the seven principles that will help it function well, how do you move towards actual practice? This section looks at three areas for you to consider as you move forward to starting the work of the MSP. It delves deeper into the scope of facilitation when different stakeholders come together: How can you help the MSP run smoothly and efficiently in practice? Where does facilitation start and where does it end? We then outline four human dimensions that are essential components of success. Finally, we look at the practical requirements for organising an MSP: what support structures will you need, how will you deal with funding issues, and how you should communicate with those outside the MSP.

Partnership broker

Facilitator

Boundary spanning

Free actor

Chair

enabler

Bridging agent

Network weaver

Community organizer

Champion

Change agent

Learning accelerator

The 'invisible' hand

Interlocutor

(art of) hosting

Convenor

Workshop facilitation

*Terms often
used to describe
a facilitator*

Facilitation

If you close your eyes and think about a facilitator… what image comes to mind? There is a good chance you were thinking about someone who leads a workshop. What we want to show you is how much broader the role can be, and how a good facilitator can contribute to the success of an MSP. At CDI, we often find it useful to demystify the concept. Rather than 'facilitator', we talk about roles and responsibilities within an MSP that can be taken up by different people with different skills.

What does a facilitator do?

Facilitation has been called an art, a science, and a skill – and all three rolled into one.[1] Recent research suggests that successful facilitators are often active bridging agents,[2] interlocutors,[3] or innovation brokers[4] who have a certain gravitas in their specialist area and are respected and trusted. Good facilitators generally know what they are talking about; they have a technical knowledge of the domain and a network they can mobilise. If these people organise a meeting, you'll want to be there – otherwise, you might miss something.

This does not make it easier to define what a facilitator does. A facilitator can play many roles including providing visionary leadership, nurturing a network, getting things organised, selling a new idea, creating space for dialogue, and running effective meetings. All of these can be summarised in three main roles: convenor, moderator, and catalyst (adapted from Sørensen and Torfing 2013).[5] If these roles are filled in an MSP, they can overcome many barriers to collaborative innovation.

A convenor brings together the relevant actors and stimulates interaction. A convenor…
- plays a key role in identifying key stakeholders and motivating them to participate in the MSP;
- clarifies the role of different stakeholders by drawing up a process map that delineates who participates, when, and how in the different phases of the MSP;
- encourages interaction and exchange between stakeholders, emphasising that everybody depends on each other's resources;
- secures political support for the objective of the MSP; and
- helps to give direction to the MSP and align the goals and expectations of stakeholders.

A moderator gets the stakeholders to collaborate by managing their differences and supporting processes of mutual learning. The idea is that the sum will be more than the parts. A moderator…
- makes collaboration easy, by arranging good and effective meetings, ensuring smooth communication, and stimulating stakeholders to contribute more (if needed);
- builds and maintains trust between the stakeholders by creating venues for informal social interaction, creating clear common ground rules, and displaying trust in the stakeholders;

- develops a common understanding through a common knowledge base, joint fact-finding missions, and a common language based on shared definitions;
- resolves or mediates conflicts so that they become constructive rather than destructive; and
- removes practical obstacles to collaboration by securing support from the management of participating stakeholders, and negotiating how stakeholders will share the costs and benefits of the MSP outcomes.

A catalyst stimulates stakeholders to think outside the box and develop and implement new and bold solutions. A catalyst...
- creates a sense of urgency either by invoking a 'burning ship' or showing that there is a 'window of opportunity';
- prevents tunnel vision by encouraging stakeholders to change their perspective, including new and different stakeholders in the team, or bringing new and inspiring knowledge to the group;
- enhances creativity in the discussions by changing the way stakeholders interact and collaborate; and
- ensures that stakeholders become ambassadors for the MSP and disseminate knowledge about the new initiatives that are developed.

See Section 4, Principle 6: Promote collaborative leadership

Can one person ever fulfil all these roles? Well, at CDI, we have yet to meet one. However, we have seen MSPs thriving because all these roles were fulfilled in an excellent way by teams. This is another reminder of how important it is for MSPs to actively nurture good teamwork. At CDI, we usually create facilitation teams, ideally including a mix of women and men from different or complementary cultural and professional backgrounds.

A facilitator is...

CONVENOR
Brings actors together
Spurs interaction
Obtains political support

CATALYST
Creates sense of urgency
Stimulates actors to think outside the box
Develops/implements new, bold situations

MODERATOR
Gets stakeholders to collaborate
Manages differences
Engages in mutual learning

Check: When your organisation is looking for an external facilitator for your MSP, be wary of consultants who offer to take on the whole responsibility. A consultant who insists on co-facilitating with others (for example stakeholders or a (local) consultant) is more likely to have understood the true scope of facilitation.

Choosing a facilitator

As discussed above, 'facilitation' really refers to a range of activities that help the MSP develop and progress smoothly, generally grouped under convening, moderating, and catalysing. These activities are usually carried out by an individual or group – the facilitators – who can be external or internal. It can be useful at times for a given MSP to have a neutral external facilitator with a wide range of skills and experience to help guide development. However, we have found that this is not always effective or realistic. Sometimes it will be useful to look at the facilitation role more as a function that can be dispersed amongst a number of people, including key stakeholders in the process and people who don't think of themselves as facilitation experts. It is important to consider the different functions and to allocate them to specific persons – but who these are will depend on the specific situation.

The main alternatives you should look at are
· individual or group,
· outsiders or insiders, and
· specialists or non-specialists.

Individual or group? You should look carefully at the advantages and disadvantages of having a single facilitator or a group, and remember that this may change over time. You might choose to have a single person for the role of, moderator, and a number of individuals for the roles of convenor and catalyst, or a different division. With a single facilitator, the responsibility is clear and easily recognised. And it is easier for a single person to have an overview of what is going on and what needs to happen, and to ensure coherence. But it can be exhausting for one person (depending on the scale of the MSP). Even worse, the process might appear to be led entirely by that person – to be their personal project and responsibility – rather than by the participants. Group facilitation can help guard against such problems and offers a greater diversity of skills, views, and capacities. But more facilitators means more time and effort to coordinate and ensure coherence.

Outsiders or insiders? Again, you need to consider the advantages and disadvantages of having an independent professional facilitator contracted by one of the stakeholders, by the MSP secretariat, or by someone already involved in the MSP.

[When starting an MSP] "it is important that convenors have both convening power in their own right and the capacity to form alliances. Especially in situations of deep divisions and distrust, it may be necessary to create a convening group that is representative of all sides and that, in effect, models the openness to dialogue it is trying to promote". - Thomas and Pruitt (2007, p. 99)

Outsiders may be able to detach themselves better from the content of discussions and focus on the process, and there will be less suspicion that they are 'taking sides'. But in general, it is the stakeholders who will mobilise interest, and at least this aspect of facilitation may be done better by an insider. An insider is likely to have a rich insight into the situation, and will also be especially motivated to make change happen. Although they may be biased, most people can learn the skill of separating their interests from the needs of the process.

When insiders act as facilitators, people may doubt they have sufficient neutrality to lead or facilitate the MSP successfully. And true neutrality is, in fact, a myth. You, as a facilitator, will usually represent or be associated with a particular stakeholder group. The key is not so much to be neutral, but to maintain integrity. Be explicit about your own background, but make sure that you empathise with all sides represented; this will help people to value you as a professional with integrity.

See Section 4, Principle 5: Communicate effectively

Specialists or generalists? Undoubtedly, there are some special skills involved in facilitating, as well as a set of personal attitudes and behaviours that are needed. Many of these can be learned, at least to some extent, but not everyone is equally able or interested. A professional specialist facilitator is likely to have a depth of experience in a wide range of contexts, which helps him or her to keep calm in difficult moments, to maintain an overview of a complex situation, and to try out different approaches when the situation is stalling. Yet leaving facilitation to the specialists again brings the risk of stakeholders giving up ownership and blaming the facilitator for setbacks. Stakeholders also need to acquire facilitation skills and experience, as this could be very useful to support long-term collaboration. It helps if the facilitation team possesses process expertise as well as content expertise. Content expertise is important to make sure that stakeholders discuss the right issues, and that the decisions and actions they agree will be effective in addressing the MSP issue. But it can be hard to find process and content expertise combined in one person, which underlines the importance once again of working with facilitation teams rather than individuals.

There is no one ideal approach to facilitation. The best approach for a particular situation will depend on the context, the issue, and the resources available. In general, we suggest working with facilitation teams that combine some of the above possibilities (insiders and outsiders, specialists and non-specialists, process and content experts). But it needs to be realistic – all the members of the MSP need to be willing to cooperate, and resources should be available to support the group. The most important point is that facilitators are aware of the diverse requirements of facilitation, and prepared to deal with them.

Facilitation competencies[6]

What does a policymaker interested in initiating an interactive policy process need to know and be able to do? What does the leader of a social activist organisation interested in initiating dialogue between groups in conflict need to know and be able to do? What does a professional facilitator employed to support an MSP need to know and be able to do? What attitudes and ethical positions will make these people more or less effective in working with different stakeholder groups?

Competence means the combination of knowledge, skills, and attitudes in a particular area. Facilitators for MSPs need six main areas of competence for designing and facilitating MSPs, regardless of the specific role (convenor, moderator, catalyst).

Understanding the context. We often hear people debate whether facilitators should be knowledgeable about the issues at hand. If they are, they will have opinions about the issues, and that can create challenges in terms of neutrality in the process and being trusted by all stakeholders. However, we have never seen a well-designed and facilitated process in which facilitators were not informed about the MSP context. A facilitator needs at least to be familiar with the main vocabulary; the pros and cons of the problem; the key characteristics of the relevant stakeholders, such as their worldviews, interests, and theories of change; and the main (power) dynamics in the system. However, the more knowledge we have, the more important it is to demonstrate neutrality by communicating transparently about our opinions and how we are keeping them out of the process.

Knowing and developing yourself. Self-awareness is essential when you are operating in a multi-stakeholder environment, and a facilitator requires significant levels of individual development. Self-awareness includes awareness of your own characteristics and behavioural tendencies, particularly when discussing with others. You need to be aware of how others react to you and of your own assumptions, feelings, and blind spots. Essentially, we use ourselves to connect with participants, model authentic communication and get to know individuals, groups, and issues that may affect us deeply. Individual development is necessary in order to evoke trust and trustworthiness, authenticity, flexibility, honesty, goal orientation, a keen sense of justice, and empathy from all participants. Individual development also helps us not to fear conflict, crisis, protests, or expressions of distrust, and enables us to turn these into opportunities for reflection and creative problem solving. In our experience, these rather psychological aspects of the work are often overlooked. Yet they are essential if MSPs are to succeed – and equally essential in protecting facilitators from exhaustion and burnout.

See Section 4, Principle 5: Communicate effectively

Envisioning the process. A facilitator needs to be able to imagine (and where relevant, design) the whole of the MSP over time, taking into account the overall system and the dynamics within and without. Envisioning an MSP includes being able to consider whole systems as well as social groups, institutions and structures, the individuals within them, and all the interrelations between such entities. Short- and long-term thinking and planning, and the ability to communicate and encourage these are vital. Many facilitators cultivate a profound understanding of the dialogue approach as a way to connect and collaborate with individuals, groups, and cultures. They move between different perspectives and worldviews, exemplifying role taking, and understanding the benefits of conversations that foster shared understanding and allow new solutions to be generated.

Understanding epistemology. Epistemology is the branch of philosophy concerned with the nature and scope of knowledge – what knowledge is, how it is acquired, and what 'truth' is. Each person approaches an MSP from the perspective of what is true for him or her. But no one, including the facilitator, can claim to hold 'the truth'. This basic epistemological assumption underpins MSPs. Our viewpoints depend on our position and roles in society; they are all valid, even though they are different. Recognising and accepting that there are different truths held by different stakeholders will help participants to build commitment to the process and respect one another. The challenge for the MSP is to learn how to respect each stakeholder's truth while creating integrated solutions. As a facilitator, you will need to design a process towards that goal, proposing plans, methods, and agendas. It is likely that your 'truth' will also be questioned.

See Section 4, Principle 2, Perspective 2: Systems thinking with the iceberg

You will need to be able to share the reasoning behind the process design – and to explain why sometimes meetings should be closed, who stakeholders should work in small groups first, why separate task forces are needed, or why draft agreements should be discussed line by line.

Choosing methods and tools. Methods and tools are what we use to transform our understanding and design of the MSP into practice. The facilitation literature is full of creative ideas, and new ideas are being developed all the time. Section 6 describes 60 tools that can be used in different phases of an MSP, including tools for identifying stakeholders, exploring issues, and developing commitment and solutions. As a facilitator, you need to know what is available and be able to select and use appropriate tools for particular activities. On the basis that form follows function, purpose and desired outcome should guide your choice of tools, while the context and framework conditions dictate what can be done.

Working in teams. There are many reasons why facilitation is best done by groups. All the competencies described above are needed to design and facilitate successful MSPs, but they don't have to be all held by a single individual: a group of people with a combination of these competencies can also make a successful team. By sharing tasks, people learn more intensely from each other. We have often observed how stakeholders and experts pick up facilitation methods and hone their skills during an MSP and by working with a process professional. But it is essential that everyone have the ability and the competence to work as part of a team. Facilitators who view facilitation as some kind of magician's trick may find it difficult to share their competencies freely and bring them into a mix with other members of the team. Some facilitators have a strong drive to be centre stage, and a desire to remain needed. Neither is helpful in an MSP's core team, which again highlights the importance of self-awareness and individual development.

The human dimension

We have identified four important human dimensions that play an essential part in the success of MSPs. As you put your MSP theories into practice, you will need to ensure that these are in place to give your MSP the best chance of achieving its goals. Like the seven principles and the process model, these dimensions – critical and informed analysis, trust, emotional engagement, and creativity – need to be actively managed. If the seven principles are the main ingredients of your soup, these four human dimensions are the spices that will determine the taste.

Critical and informed analysis

No matter how good the organisation, an MSP can be compromised by poor analysis. This doesn't mean that you need more scientists in the MSP. Rather, you need to look at ways to improve the quality of critical and informed analysis. This can involve science, but don't underestimate the analysis that the stakeholders can produce themselves.

There are three ways in which lack of analysis can weaken an MSP.
Not enough critical analysis. If participants join an MSP but don't know enough about the topic, they will find it hard to arrive at new insights. When organisations send the wrong representatives, or keep sending new staff without proper briefing or handover, the MSP can easily end up repeating yesterday's discussions and forgetting new conclusions, and can lose credibility. One approach you can use to avoid this is to carry out scoping studies prior to your MSP events and summarise the results in short issue briefs. You also need to take care to identify, invite, and get commitment from, people with the appropriate knowledge – which is one of the keys to a successful process. This is not done by sending general invitation letters to organisations: you should discuss it with people you know before suggesting or deciding who to invite, and engage with individuals face-to-face before the events.

Not enough independent analysis. Efforts to coordinate stakeholders can easily end in arguments with groups taking fixed and opposing positions. One party states that the core of the problem is X (backed up by their own case study); the other party then responds that, while X is indeed an issue, it is in fact caused by Y (backed up by their own research), implying that they can't do anything about it. The stakeholders retreat to fixed positions with no opportunity for true dialogue. In situations like this, suggest commissioning independent research to analyse the situation and the claims made by stakeholders, and ask stakeholders to wait for the results before taking decisions.

See Section 4,
Principle 4:
Deal with
conflict

Not enough joint analysis. Even when studies are completed and all the data is available, getting to decisions can be challenging. You will need to organise joint learning activities and fact-finding missions that enable stakeholders to explore the issue and develop new perspectives together. Fostering

See Section
4, Principle 7:
Foster
participatory
learning

participatory learning will improve the analytical level of discussions and help stakeholders get to know each other and develop trust.

The golden rule is to involve all stakeholders in analysis. Try to actively involve the weaker stakeholders, for example using action-oriented research (AOR).[7] This will build ownership and commitment from these stakeholders, and can also empower them to voice their concerns more effectively.

Trust

"Trust comes on foot, but leaves on horseback". This quote is attributed to Johan Thorbecke, the Dutch politician responsible for the first constitution of the Netherlands in 1848. If stakeholders have trust in each other, or in the process they are engaging in, they will be more willing to accept uncertainties. After all, if the vegetable seller in the market knows I have kept my word to her in the past, she will be more inclined to give me the mangos – even if I have forgotten my purse.

Lack of trust is probably the most frequently cited reason for breakdown in an MSP. Trust doesn't just come from warm personal feelings. You and the stakeholders can actively help to build trust by acting appropriately. Ensuring that others have the freedom to present their concerns, and listening to and honouring these concerns, can be key – as can acknowledging the legitimacy of other people's goals, even if they differ from your own.[8] Good quality dialogue will help to build trust because it allows partners to move beyond their stereotypes of each other, while still respecting each other's identities.

One indicator of low trust in MSPs is the speed at which stakeholders start talking about formalising the collaboration. A discussion that quickly turns to contracts, Memoranda of Understanding (MoUs), and budget allocation could indicate lack of trust. It can be dangerous to frame the MSP around formalities at an early stage when relationships are just developing. In general, you should invest time in creating a joint vision or conduct a joint activity before talking about contracts.

Trust can disappear quickly even after it has been carefully built. A successful event organised by a multi-stakeholder initiative in the Netherlands was followed by unexpected turmoil. The reason: one stakeholder had reported the event on its website without using the logos of the other organising partners. It took several months to win back the trust that had so quickly evaporated. The lesson for the future was to make specific agreements on how to communicate about joint activities.

FROM DESIGN TO PRACTICE

But notions of trust differ from culture to culture, and you should take this into account, too. In regions with high levels of bureaucracy, such as West Africa, it is common to discuss formal contracts and MoUs before stakeholders actually do something together. In this case, dealing with formalities is part of understanding the issue at hand, not necessarily an indicator of low trust. Trust in Western societies is often based on informal relationships, while in many Asian societies trust only develops when there is evidence that the other person has done what they promised.[9]

See Section 6: Tools to connect

Difficult conflicts can be a real driver of learning and engagement. But people need to experience respect, openness, and trust to move through such conflict.

Emotional engagement

People will only put in the time and effort needed – the commitment – to make the MSP successful if they are emotionally engaged. Emotional engagement – the sense that it really matters – can come from our deeper convictions and beliefs about certain issues (such as a desire for justice, peace, and wholeness). It can also come from more down-to-earth incentives: that joining an MSP is part of the job you love to do, is good for your career, or that your boss just loves it. Two types of engagement are important in an MSP. One is the individual engagement of participants and facilitators; the other is the commitment of the whole group to work, learn, and innovate together.

Individual engagement. Collaboration not only requires commitment, but also entails genuine readiness for change, which is quite rare.[10] Where does engagement come from? Otto Scharmer and Katrin Kaufer[11] describe three openings needed to transform systems: opening the mind (to challenge our assumptions), opening the heart (to be vulnerable and to truly hear one another), and opening the will (to let go of pre-set goals and agendas and see what is really needed and possible).[12] To engage with systemic change, you need to see yourself as part of the system that needs to change, rather than thinking that you need to change others.[13] An NGO leader in Cambodia told us that he could only engage with government officials after he suspended his judgement of government practices. His assumptions about government officials had

Creating a positive learning environment. A Change of Scene

"CDI and KIT have been helping Dutch Embassies to improve their country programmes with partners. In Ghana, learning and reflection was always considered important – but embassy staff rarely attended reflection sessions or learning workshops. So we organised field trips, where embassy staff would go to project sites with their partners and interview stakeholders, which led to heated debates in the bus. Going on a journey, experiencing a change of scene, engaging with real problems, and making new connections yielded more learning than the office-based meetings. Although this sounds effortless, it involved a lot of prior planning and thoughtful debriefing to make the learning 'stick' and apply it to policy". - Thea Hilhorst KIT

prevented him listening and being able to think outside the box. People who excel in engagement have realised not only that the world needs to change – but also that they need to change.

Engagement as a group. People who are engaged are also open to learning, which is an important component of MSP success. It is useful to think about how emotional reactions can block or motivate engagement and learning. Feelings of confidence, inspiration, compassion, calmness, joy, and empowerment will all encourage people to engage. Feelings of fear, frustration, anxiety, anger, and irritation will block engagement. Engagement can be driven by a sense of urgency or even crisis, but if the feeling of crisis is too great, people may become paralysed by anxiety or fear. The MSP facilitation should aim to develop a safe environment in which stakeholders feel able to branch out into unchartered territory, despite the potential for discomfort.

Creativity

In recent decades, we have learned much more about how the human mind processes information.[14] We now know that learning can be considerably strengthened by the creative use of visual images, art, music, and drama. Often, the most essential things that stakeholders want to communicate to other stakeholders are not facts or political positions. Rather, they are about norms (standards of behaviour), beliefs (assumptions about the way things are), and values (standards of importance). It can be very difficult to express these in words. Sometimes, a song, a picture, or a play can express what can't be said. For example:
· After indigenous representatives in Honduras shared songs and poems on what the forest meant to them, the representatives of a mining company and government realised how deep the sense of belonging to the physical place really was for these people.
· After playing the role of a government civil servant dealing with a corrupt politician in a role-play, an NGO worker realised the impossible dilemmas that public sector officials sometimes face.
· After making a drawing of an ideal future, a quiet academic was able to share his fears about environmental degradation with a group of policymakers.

Diversity and creativity seem to be closely linked.[15] Groups of stakeholders become more creative if they are diverse, and they make better decisions.[16] They have a variety of backgrounds, knowledge, and worldviews, which provide more options for discussion and a broader basis for understanding. But the diversity also needs to be well managed to avoid misunderstanding and confusion.

Stimulating creativity among stakeholders can greatly enhance learning and innovative practice. It can also add a fun element – but be careful as not everyone has the same definition of fun. Still, bringing people slightly outside of their comfort zone is a good way to help them look, feel, and behave differently towards each other and the issue at hand. And that is where innovative ideas can strike.

Getting organised

You will need to make many operational decisions once your MSP gets going. People naturally incline towards replicating what they know. But an MSP is different from most organisations, and often requires different procedures and structures to the businesses, NGOs, and government organisations that stakeholders are familiar with. Think about the seven principles discussed in Section 4. Operational decisions should be guided by values of fairness, transparency, and legitimacy. The five particular areas you should look at during the operational phase are support structures, strategic guidance, accountability, funding, and communication.

Support structures

During the Initiating Phase, an MSP usually has limited resources and individuals work from their own organisational bases. As the MSP develops, it may need more practical support for organising meetings, doing research, developing networks, and coordinating projects. And you will need to decide how to structure this support. One possibility is for the MSP to be hosted by a lead agency so it can benefit from the agency's support systems. The potential disadvantage is that the association with the agency will be too strong. Stakeholders could also decide to establish an independent initiative or platform in the form of a secretariat, initiative, backbone organisation, or forum.[17] This has the advantage of being equally distant to all partners, but risks the platform becoming a force of its own. Another possibility is to have a decentralized system, an open alliance, in which support functions are distributed among partners. Whatever the decision, the outcome must be agreed by all the main stakeholders, or support for the MSP will dwindle and its legitimacy will be questioned.

Strategic guidance

Some MSPs find it useful to have formalised oversight from a board, committee, or support group, in addition to guidance from the core group of facilitators. This oversight group plays a different role to the board of a normal type of organisation as an MSP usually has limited legal responsibility. Here, the role is more to provide inspiration, make networks available to the MSP, bring in new stakeholder groups, provide inputs to the strategy, and generally raise the MSP's profile. The role is also defined by the mandate that the MSP can carve out for itself: is it linked to any formal (inter)governmental decision making? What authority and legal status can it attain?

Accountability

What may start as an organic, informal collaboration between stakeholders usually develops into a more formal structure. This is inevitable, and usually healthy. The success of an MSP is based on its ability to deliver on its ambitions, and this means that decision making, management, and development arrangements need to be appropriate and effective. Whether formal or informal is better depends on the situation. The Partnering Toolbook[18] provides a tool to help you work through the pros and cons of different structures.

See Section 6, Tool 38: Partnering Agreement

As the MSP moves from the Initiating to the Adaptive Planning Phase, stakeholders will be committing increased resources, which calls for clear agreements. You need to develop a Partnering Agreement[19] at an early stage of collaboration to avoid misunderstanding. This is not a contract; it is not legally binding. This is an agreement developed between the stakeholders as equals. It outlines their agreement to cooperate, and states explicitly the interests that each stakeholder has. Legally binding contracts may be made later if MSPs enter into complex implementation arrangements or handle large amounts of funding.

Funding

MSPs will require funding to act upon their ambitions: stakeholders need to meet, they need to prepare for these meetings, they need to consult with their constituents, and capacities within or around the stakeholders need to be developed. Conversations shouldn't start with money matters, but they are a reality to be dealt with.

See Section 6: Tools for connecting and Tools for commitment

In practice, we see many stakeholders being drawn to MSPs because they see a possibility for funding. This is not always a bad reason. But if it is the dominant motivation, it can harm the collaboration. Competition for financial resources is normal, and it is naive to expect stakeholders to choose for the 'benefit of the whole group' at the expense of their own organisational interests. The facilitators should prioritise activities that help people realise that what they can achieve together as an MSP can also help them realise their own personal/ organisational goals as part of the process design.

Participants should preferably have no direct role in funding the process they are involved in. If individual stakeholders are directly funding the activities, the power relationships in the MSP can become distorted. If possible, use an independent agency or a purpose-built trust to ensure that money administration is delinked from those who have a direct stake in the outcomes of the MSP.[20]

Tip: Hiring a graphic facilitator or graphic recorder can enhance the creativity of stakeholders at a meeting. See for example http://en.wikipedia.org/wiki/Graphic_facilitation or www.imagethink.net/ or www.theworldcafe.com/pdfs/graphicBenefits.pdf

Communication

See Section 4,
Principle 5

Principle 5 says to communicate effectively. This doesn't just mean good communication between stakeholders. Facilitators need to guide stakeholders in communicating with those not immediately involved in the MSP discussions: the stakeholders' constituencies, second tier stakeholders, and the general public.

The MSP should draw up a communication plan for different external audiences. Given the high stakes involved, the sensitivities around communication are immense – whether it refers to success or failure. Stakeholders will often disagree about the right moment to 'go public' with decisions that have been made. And what some stakeholders call a historic success may not even be thought of as news by others. Talking the walk[21] by McManus and Tennyson provides extensive guidance on how to organise communication inside and outside MSPs.

The Partnering Agreement should include procedures for what is recorded, who needs to approve reports or communiqués, and how information is disseminated. The overall principle should be that whatever can be made public should be, unless stakeholders explicitly specify why certain information should remain within a closed group. Facilitators can propose working under the Chatham House Rule[22] in order to provide anonymity. Finally, have a clear discussion about which logos (if any) should be included in MSP communications.

It is critically important to convene a dialogue in a way that builds public awareness and credibility, so that the process will have an impact beyond the immediate participant group.

Questions for designing and facilitating MSPs

· Are you prepared to learn and change? Ask yourself why, or why not.

· Does your current facilitation team cover the roles of convening, moderating, and catalysing? What is needed to ensure that all roles are being performed?

· Can you recall from your experience a situation where collaboration failed because of missing ingredients (critical and informed analysis; trust; emotional engagement; creativity)? How could this have been avoided?

· Are there clear agreements about how stakeholder representatives should communicate with each other and back to their constituencies and the press?

6 CHOOSING TOOLS

Methods and tools are what we use to transform our understanding and design of the MSP into practice. They will play an essential role in shaping your MSP, helping individuals to become part of a cohesive and productive group, and releasing creativity and innovation. We have included this section on tools partly because the most frequent questions we are asked are, "Do you know a good tool for situation X?" or "Can you share your toolbox with me?" But when you think about tools, remember that the tools themselves are less important than the spirit and context in which they are used. In the following, we introduce some general ideas about the tools and methodologies, followed by summaries of 60 different tools as an overview of what's available.

Tools per stage:

CONNECTION

1 Introductions
2 Human Spectrogram
3 Rich Picture
4 Semi-structured Interviews
5 Stakeholder Identification
6 Appreciative Story Telling
7 Questionnaires; Surveys
8 Problem Definition
   Worksheet
9 Ground Rules

CO-CREATION

34 Tuckman
35 Belbin Team Roles
36 Scenario Planning
37 Conflict Styles
38 Partnering Agreements
39 Open Space
40 Document and
   Summarise
41 Visioning
42 Circle of Coherence

SHARED LANGUAGE

10 Stakeholder Characteristics and Roles Matrix
11 NetMapping
12 Stakeholder Analysis
13 World Café
14 Problem Tree
15 Timeline
16 Force Field Analysis
17 In Context Immersions
18 SWOT Analysis
19 Delphi
20 Visual Reminders
21 Cynefin Framework
22 Friends and Strangers
23 Trendline
24 Four Quadrants of Change

CONVERGENCE

43 Prototyping
44 Prioritising and Ranking
45 Comparing Proposals
46 Feedback from
   Stakeholders
47 Ritual Dissent
48 Card Clustering
49 Socratic Dialogue
50 A Change of Scene
51 Silence

DIVERGENCE

25 Adjust Group Size
26 Role Plays
27 Forms of Power
28 Six Thinking Hats
29 Multiple Perspectives
30 Power Ranking
31 Guided Fantasy
32 Five Colours of Change
33 Combining Ideas That
   Might Work Together

COMMITMENT

52 Set Decision Rules
53 Make a Visual Theory
   of Change
54 Polls
55 Fish Bowl
56 Reflection
57 Synthesis
58 Option One-and-a-Half
59 Closing Circle
60 Evaluation

CHOOSING TOOLS

Why do we need tools?

Just caring about a challenge is not enough for people to remain successfully engaged in an MSP. We have to maximise the opportunities for different people to find a voice in the process, and to keep it fresh and interesting for all. This means using different methodologies from different sources at each stage in the process. At CDI, we draw heavily on our experience in participatory development, but we also take inspiration from other domains including scientific research, business design thinking, dialogue, MSP practice, and creative artistic expression.

One of the core tasks of a facilitator trying to bring stakeholders together is integrating their different perspectives. This means making sure that everyone understands where the others are coming from and why – not that everyone needs to agree. This is not easy: sometimes the incompatibility in the interests and mental models of those involved is just too great. Imagine biophysicists, social scientists, politicians, bureaucrats, social activists, resource users, and community members in conversation. Their different worldviews won't come together easily.

This is where you need the ability to choose the right set of methodologies, tools, and attitudes to enable different actors to communicate and transcend their incompatibilities at a particular moment in time. The following questions will help you:

- **Is this the time to invest in teambuilding?** People may need to understand each other better and accept their differences before they are able to think about building on each other's strengths.
- **Is the MSP in a diverging, emerging, or converging stage?** At what stage is your process? Is your priority exploring and generating new ideas; is it analysing, refining, and choosing between options; or is it time for planning?
- **Is it time to look back, or time to look forward?** Is it time to share and reflect on past experiences in order to adapt your strategies, or is it time to consider future scenarios to create new possibilities?

Methodologies versus Tools

A methodology is a family of tools, usually linked through a theoretical perspective or framework. A tool is a practical short-term help to achieve a certain task. For example, Appreciative Inquiry (AI) is a methodology, but Appreciative Story Telling is a tool that belongs to the AI family.

- **Should you deliberately address power imbalances?** How might power relations and conflict dynamics within the group of stakeholders play out when different approaches are used? For instance, highly stylised processes, such as a formal debate and ritualised or time-constrained contributions, can require a lot of effort, but can also be quite effective in levelling participants and de-personalising the issues.
- **What is culturally and politically appropriate?** For instance, should you choose methodologies that give people used to playing a background role – marginalised people, women, the young – a greater chance of feeling comfortable voicing their thoughts, rather than exposing them to a more challenging format?

Where do the tools come from?

See Section 4, Principle 1: Systemic change

Participatory learning and action is an umbrella term for a wide range of participatory methodologies focusing on full participation of people in the processes of learning about their needs and opportunities and carrying out actions to address them. The methodologies include Participatory Rural Appraisal (PRA), which uses visualisation and group-based analysis of community issues; Rapid Appraisal of Agricultural Knowledge Systems (RAAKS),[1] which focuses on generating and sharing knowledge between stakeholders for innovation in rural development; and the soft systems methodology.

Large-scale group interventions are a family of methodologies from organisational development (OD). It includes Open Space, Future Search, Technology of Participation, and Appreciative Inquiry. All of these offer multi-session processes to analyse, design, decide, and implement with groups that are fully engaged.[2]

Design thinking refers to a range of methodologies from the world of business and social innovation that focus on ways to develop innovations with stakeholders and users. These methodologies emphasise creativity, systems analysis, and concrete results, and include Human Centred Design from IDEO,[3] and methodologies developed by innovators such as NESTA[4] and SiG.[5]

Dialogue is a catch-all name for the methodologies and tools that have sprung from professionals and volunteers active in peace building, reconciliation, and dialogue processes. These methodologies are particularly strong in bringing stakeholders with opposing views together to talk a way out of deadlock and create perspectives for a better future. They include Democratic Dialogue and the methods developed by organisations such as Dialogos and the National Coalition for Dialogue and Deliberation (NCDD)[6].

More information can be found on www.mspguide.org

CHOOSING TOOLS

Tools fit for purpose

In the following, we offer you 60 process tools serving different purposes. Even this large number, is just a sample of the hundreds of tools available; we have chosen these because they are the ones we find especially useful to support MSP processes. The tools mostly derive from families of methodologies as outlined in the box.

We have grouped the tools by six purposes – connection, issue exploration and shared language, divergence, co-creation, convergence, and commitment – inspired by the work of Sam Kaner[7] and the Rockefeller Foundation's GATHER guide.[8] These purposes often coincide with a particular MSP stage: connecting, for example, will usually happen at the start.[9]

Some tools speak to the rational mind: these will help participants analyse the issue and see the connections. Others speak more to the intuitive mind: they will help participants express mental models and feelings, tapping into participants' (often unrecognised) creative and empathetic reservoirs. Finally, there are tools that cater to the 'we' of MSPs: managing group dynamics, and dealing with power issues, conflicts, and inclusiveness.

CONNECTION

SHARED LANGUAGE

DIVERGENCE

Each part has an overview of the purpose followed by brief summaries of individual tools with the approximate time needed and a star rating for difficulty. Details of sources are given in the endnote references. The summaries are just a guide; you can find detailed descriptions of each tool on the MSP portal at www.mspguide.org. You can use the tools as described or adapt them to suit your purpose. And you can use them to clarify your own thinking and prepare for your work with stakeholders, as well as in the MSP itself. Many tools can be used for multiple purposes. For example, Six Thinking Hats can be used both for the divergence stage and during the convergence stage; in general, we have placed them under the purpose where they are most commonly used.

Six commonly used stages

There are no hard and fast rules for how to structure the blank slate of your MSP agenda. But most well-designed MSP processes are structured around a particular series of stages. The event begins with connection, establishes a shared language, and then present a divergent set of views on the topic. Depending on the MSP's purpose, that divergence may be followed by the co-creation of new ideas, convergence on a certain set of answers, or even commitment to take action.

CO-CREATION

CONVERGENCE

COMMITMENT

Connection: Defining the issue and becoming a group

Even when participants know the agenda, they are often not clear about what they are expected to do and what the group hopes to accomplish. Tools to get started are really important: they help people orient themselves ("Where am I in this group?") and open up ("What can I contribute?"), and set the scene for constructive dialogue. They are also used to gather background information for the MSP.

At this stage, your aim is get as many people as possible talking to each other. Participants will listen more if they have been able to talk and share themselves and feel that they know some of the others.

One of the key outcomes should be that everybody is clear what the issue is. You will need to use entry-level analytical exercises that help participants think about the content. They will discover that people have different perspectives on the issue, and will realise how many learning and networking opportunities there are. As a facilitator, you need to help the group to frame the issue well. Different participants will have different interests, but at this stage, it is only important to make sure that the issue itself is clear. Make sure that participants also know what is not (yet) on the agenda for discussion.

■ Individual: fairly simple self-administered tool
■ Interaction required: requires interaction with colleagues / partners
■ Complex: needs preparation time and skilled facilitation
∗ Grades in difficulty

TOOL 1

Introductions

At the start of meetings, carry out an activity that allows everybody to know who is in the room and establishes a sense of group identity. It sets the tone for how you want to engage people. Don't make it too personal or hilarious, as people might be hesitant in a new setting.

15–45 minutes ★★☆☆☆

TOOL 2

Human Spectrogram (or Dancefloor)

Describe opposing perspectives at two ends of a spectrum and ask participants to line up along the line to show where they stand. This helps to surface similarities and differences in a group, and for people to get to know each other.

15–30 minutes ★☆☆☆☆

TOOL 3

Rich Picture[10]

Joint visualisation of cases in small groups (5–7). This helps to quickly share and understand the actors, factors, and relationships affecting the issue at hand. The end product is a flipchart full of symbols, drawings, and arrows that depicts the issue, made by all.

60–90 minutes ★★☆☆☆

TOOL 4

Semi-structured Interviews

As opposed to closed surveys with fixed questions, a semi-structured interview is open, allowing new ideas to be brought up during the interview as a result of what the interviewee says. This can be an initial activity to scope an issue with different stakeholders, or used at a later stage for in-depth enquiry.

several weeks ★★★☆☆

TOOL 5

Stakeholder Identification

Fast visual overview of the most relevant stakeholders for the issue at hand, and their relationships. Possibilities include a Venn diagram or Spider web network analysis.

40–65 minutes ★★☆☆☆

TOOL 6

Appreciative Story Telling

Participants interview one another about their contribution to the MSP. Focus on rediscovering and reorganising the good rather than problem solving. Also helps to practice active listening skills.

60 minutes ★★☆☆☆

TOOL 7

Questionnaires; Surveys

To validate the need for an MSP, find out more details on the nature of the issue, or set a joint baseline. Remember that doing surveys respectfully demands preparation and well-trained enumerators. Online tools can improve design, dissemination, and analysis. Needs a qualified research team.

several months ★★★★☆

TOOL 8

Problem Definition Worksheet[11]

This worksheet helps to clarify which problem you are working on by asking five questions. It will cause people to focus ideas in the same direction. Can be used individually or as a way to structure group discussions.

1 hour ★★☆☆☆

TOOL 9

Ground Rules

Discuss principles for how the group wants to interact. The rules should cover such topics as how to behave in meetings (phone and computer use), and the norms for communicating what has been discussed beyond the room (confidentiality).

20 minutes ★★☆☆☆

Shared language: Understanding the issue and appreciating different perspectives

After being introduced to each other and to the issue, it is time for participants to dive into the details. These tools can help you perform further analysis and open up the conversation to allow different perspectives to be voiced.

At this stage, you will discover how well participants can articulate their understanding of the issue. You will also notice individual capacity gaps that you need to address so that everyone can participate meaningfully. You can help by mixing people up (allowing the new people to absorb knowledge from more experienced participants) or by creating separate groups which can discuss on different scales (e.g. 'field people' and 'policy people').

Many of the tools described are analytical. They will help you to question the issue more deeply and use all the perspectives in the room to complement and add to the picture being built up. We find that academically and non-academically trained participants can happily contribute together to an analysis if you choose the right tool. For example, 'policy people' can find it very inspiring and motivating to engage in conversations with 'field people'. But make sure that there is also time for policy people and field people to deliberate separately from each other and digest their impressions amongst themselves.

Focus on emphasising the common ground among participants and avoid choosing tools or summarising discussions in a way that emphasises the differences. The contrasts will become visible later anyway. At this point, you want to instil a sense of common purpose by sharing information and creating a new 'container' together. You also want to construct a solid knowledge base that participants can use to start developing solutions.

TOOL 10

Stakeholder Characteristics and Roles Matrix

Small groups can fill out this matrix to systematically analyse the most important stakeholders, their stakes, what they can contribute to the success of the MSP, and whether they are influential or not.

60 minutes ✴✴✴✴

TOOL 14

Problem Tree

This helps to find solutions by mapping out the anatomy of cause and effect around an issue. By asking 'why' many times, the underlying causes and ultimate effects can be displayed in the form of a tree. Branches are effects; roots are causes.

90 minutes ✴✴✴✴

TOOL 18

SWOT Analysis

This well-known assessment tool lists the strengths, weaknesses, opportunities, and threats of a project, partnership, or product. It helps to distinguish between factors that can and can't be influenced.

30–90 minutes ✴✴✴✴

TOOL 11

NetMapping [12]

This helps to understand and visualise how stakeholder goals work out in an MSP. List 6–8 important stakeholders, position them on a flipchart, draw out relationships (supporting/challenging), and agree on the amount of influence the stakeholders have. The more stones or beans, the more influence.

60–90 minutes ★★★✱✱

TOOL 12

Stakeholder Analysis: Importance/Influence Matrix

This captures how much influence each stakeholder has over the relevant issues or possible MSP objectives, and their level of interest in the issue. Can be used when initiating an MSP, but also to review the situation in an established MSP. It specifically helps to identify (potential) stakeholders who might not yet be on board.

60–90 minutes ★★★✱✱

TOOL 13

World Café [13]

Participants rotate among small groups to discuss different topics, building on previous conversations and sharing the results in a plenary. Up to 3 rounds. One host stays at each table for continuity.

90–120 minutes ★★★✱✱

TOOL 15

Timeline

Shows how to map moments and metrics that shaped the issue or the MSP. Make a horizontal line up to today, choose intervals (e.g. 6 months), and plot events, projects, successes, and disappointments along the line using symbols.

30–90 minutes ★★★✱✱

TOOL 16

Force Field Analysis

This helps you make a decision by analysing the forces for and against a change you want to create. Put the proposed change in the middle. Left: list the forces for change. Right: list the forces against change. How can we reduce the resisting forces? How can we capitalise on the driving forces?

60–90 minutes ★★✱✱✱

TOOL 17

In Context Immersions

Avoid talking about beneficiaries or clients in their absence. If it is inappropriate or impractical for them to join your meeting, go to meet them where they are. A one-day field visit is the minimum, and will give great spin-off in terms of team building and learning; however, it's better to stay overnight and work with the group; this provides empathy and realism about solutions. Double check logistics!

At least 1 day plus briefing and debriefing ★★★✱✱

TOOL 19

Delphi

This is a process that uses an expert panel to make complex decisions by asking the panel a question (or several), collating and summarising the replies, sending out a summary, and again asking the question. Panel members may change their response in the direction of an emerging consensus. Can be used in workshops, but often done by email iterations.

60 minutes (meeting) to 3 weeks (by email) ★★★★✱

TOOL 20

Visual Reminders

Create frameworks, diagrams, and illustrations to capture and communicate your insights about complex issues. Examples: Venn diagram, flowchart, mind map, two-by-two matrix, relationship map. You will usually find visually oriented people in your group, who listen well and can convert ideas into a visual reminder - use them.Can be done any time as part of group work or individual reflection

★✱✱✱✱

TOOL 21

Cynefin Framework [14]

This management decision tool can help determine whether the issue your MSP is addressing is obvious (simple), complicated, complex, or chaotic. The result has consequences for how to manage or intervene.

See Section 4, Principle 1 Systemic Change

60 minutes (20 intro + 40 casework) ★★★★✱

CHOOSING TOOLS

■ Individual: fairly simple   ■ Requires interaction: colleagues / partners   ■ Complex: needs preparation   ✱ Grades in difficulty

TOOL 22

Friends and Strangers

This game energises, and also illustrates how a small change in a rule can have big effects on the dynamics of a complex adaptive system. People walk around in an open space, and have to move close to a 'friend' and remain far from a 'stranger'. A second round has a small change in the rule: people have to be in between their friend and the stranger.

15 minutes ✱✱✱ ✱✱

TOOL 23

Trendline

This is used to analyse the past and present situation regarding resources, issues (e.g. position of women), and initiatives. It can also indicate a community's intentions for its future direction. Can be done with clients/beneficiaries to look at changes due to an MSP, but can also be done for the MSP as such.

60 minutes ✱✱✱✱✱

TOOL 24

Four Quadrants of Change[15]

This helps participants consider what kinds of change strategies are being used in the MSP, and which strategies might be missing. It distinguishes between personal, interpersonal, cultural, and structural entry points for change.

See Section 4, Principle 1
Systemic Change

45 minutes ✱✱✱✱✱

Divergence: Broadening perspectives on the issue and surfacing and appreciating differences

This is the stage where the differences in understanding, seeing, and valuing become visible. By this time, people will know who is holding what view, or is aligned to which camp. Now it's your task as facilitator to create a safe environment for these differences to be expressed and examined.

You don't need to smooth away the differences, or pretend they don't exist. Rather, you need to help the group to work with the conflict so that stronger solutions and commitment can be developed later. The challenge is how to encourage people to withhold their judgement and not jump to conclusions. ("These NGO people always blame us and are never constructive"; "These business people are only interested in making quick money".)

At this stage, you will need to rely on your intuition, but you should choose the tools together with others to double-check your perception of the situation. For example, if you sense that there are power issues at play that make it difficult for women to express their views, you might choose to discuss power using power analysis tools. Yet this might be too confrontational and counterproductive. An alternative could be to hold break-out groups for women to reflect on how they can contribute best.

The Divergence stage can be quite challenging and you may feel that solutions will never come. The challenge is to hold the space of not-yet-knowing and to trust your group to work through. If you arrive at easy solutions too quickly at this stage, they are unlikely to be the best.

TOOL 25
Adjust Group Size

Allow participants to have conversations rather than listening to plenary sessions using buzz and break-outs. "Please discuss in threesomes what you thought of this morning's presentations", or "Let's divide into five groups and work on question x; report back using template y".

5–90 minutes ✱✱✱✱✱

TOOL 26
Role Plays

Some participants can play the roles of key outside stakeholders and either brainstorm or offer reactions in that role. Participants can express concerns and ideas without these being directly attributed to them.

60–90 minutes ✱✱✱✱✱

TOOL 27
Forms of Power[16]

This helps participants consider what kinds of change strategies are being used in the MSP, and which strategies might be missing. It distinguishes between personal, interpersonal, cultural, and structural entry points for change.

See Section 4, Principle 1
Systemic Change

45 minutes ✱✱✱✱✱

TOOL 28
Six Thinking Hats[17]

This enables groups to look at a decision from several points of view. It involves play-acting for six types of thinking such as 'white hat thinking' (objective, neutral) or 'yellow hat thinking' (positive, constructive). From Edward DeBono.

60 minutes ✱✱✱✱✱

TOOL 29
Multiple Perspectives[18]

This helps a group to widen their perspectives: the points of view from which stakeholders regard a problem. Rotating between roles encourages the group to see an important issue from as many vantage points as possible.

60 minutes ✱✱✱✱✱

TOOL 30
Power Ranking

This helps participants realise that every person has different kinds of rank and privileges - situational, social, and personal - and that these attributes can give a certain level of power. Only use this if there is basic trust within the group. This role-play exercise generates lots of group energy.

60 minutes ✱✱✱✱✱

TOOL 31
Guided Fantasy

People are asked to close their eyes and make an imaginary journey. Related to the issue, introduce a new landscape, country, or world and ask participants to dream about what happens, who they encounter, and what their feelings are. Afterwards, share dreams in pairs and pick a few examples to share with all.

**In total 1 or 2 hours
✱✱✱✱✱**

TOOL 32
Five Colours of Change[19]

Five ways of thinking about change: yellow print, blue print, red print, green print, and white print. Each based on a family of theories about change. A test identifies the predominant colour among participants, and helps to discuss different change paradigms within the MSP.

Free online test 15 minutes, plus 1 hour debriefing and reflection ✱✱✱✱✱

TOOL 33
Combining Ideas That Might Work Together

Brainstorming is used to collect an open list of ideas without evaluating them. Then participants are invited to reflect on which combination of ideas might work.

90 minutes (first brainstorm round, individual reflection: 45 min.) second round, individual reflection followed by collection of ideas: 45 min ✱✱✱✱✱

■ Individual: fairly simple   ■ Requires interaction: colleagues / partners   ■ Complex: needs preparation   ✱ Grades in difficulty

Co-creation: Developing options to address the issue and helping people to engage and collaborate effectively

The emphasis at this stage shifts towards developing group outputs using the raw material from the previous stages. There are many different types of outputs including plans, study designs, prototypes, pathways, and solutions. As in the Divergence stage, your aim is to encourage participants to develop a range of options and to avoid deciding on a single solution or direction too early. Right now, you should ensure that the ideas of all participants are noted. Final decisions will be taken at the Convergence stage.

You will need tools to structure group collaboration and to help deliver tangible outputs. Some of the suggested tools will help people to work together, to have a dialogue rather than a monologue, and to build relationships and teams. Others support the analysis needed for developing options.

TOOL 34

Tuckman (forming, storming, norming, performing)

This model helps groups to reflect on different stages in-group formation. In order to perform as a group, groups need to move through different stages, which may include conflict.

30 minutes ★★ ✱✱✱

TOOL 35

Belbin Team Roles[20]

Participants take a 20-minute self-test to determine which role they predominantly play in teams. Results are shared and used for reflection on how teamwork can be optimised in this MSP.

See Section 4, Principle 6 Collaborative Leadership

45 minutes ★★★ ✱✱

TOOL 36

Scenario Planning

Possible futures for the MSP are developed based on two major independent driving forces that cause change. The driving forces are combined using a 2×2 matrix. The possible future in each quadrant is described by a short story. The tool stimulates creative, forward thinking.

3 hours to 3 days
★★★★ ✱

TOOL 37

Conflict Styles[21]

The group uses a test of 30 statements developed by Thomas and Kilmann to gain insight into different ways in which people respond to conflict. Strong teams have a diversity of conflict styles to cope with challenges.

30–60 minutes ★★★ ✱✱

TOOL 38

Partnering Agreements[22]

A partnering agreement, which is not legally binding, can be drawn up as a commitment to collaborate. This is a good first step in consolidating an MSP, and makes the interests of all stakeholders explicit. It can be an alternative or precursor to a contract.

3 weeks to 6 months
★★★★ ✱

TOOL 39

Open Space

Volunteers offer to lead discussion on a topic; participants join the session they are interested in (as in a market place). Encourages self-organisation within the goals of the meeting. Outputs are proposals developed by sub-groups, which are brought back to the plenary.

60–180 minutes ★★★★ ✱

TOOL 40

Document and Summarise

Ideas that are generated need to be captured and summarised in a way that other participants understand but the creators still recognise. Use templates to ensure that small groups come back with appropriate outputs.

No specific time ★ ✱✱✱✱

TOOL 41

Visioning

Create a vision answering the question: "What do we want to see in place in 5–10 years as a result of this MSP?" After reviewing the context, individuals brainstorm vision elements, which are shared, clustered, and named. Eventually all the elements are combined in one vision sentence.

60 minutes ★★ ✱✱✱

TOOL 42

Circle of Coherence[23]

This can be used to review an established MSP or network, preferably with stakeholders. The goal is to expand insight into the way a vital network functions, and to clarify participants' positions in the network. The tool helps people reflect on the vital space that keeps their MSP healthy and vibrant, and how this can be strengthened.

60 minutes ★★★★ ✱

CHOOSING TOOLS

■ Individual: fairly simple ■ Requires interaction: colleagues / partners ■ Complex: needs preparation ★ Grades in difficulty

Convergence: Deciding which ideas could work and prioritising and refining what has been created

At this stage, you should focus on creating as much shared understanding as possible, and getting a sense that progress is being made towards solutions. Many of the options generated at the co-creation stage might still be too general and need specification and testing. For example, a group may have proposed to 'include farmers in decisions that affect them', but what does that look like in practice? What needs to change? What are the implications?

These tools will help you to prototype and weigh the pros and cons of each idea. You can use some of them during meetings, but you will want to use many in activities outside meetings – like field testing and getting stakeholder feedback on ideas.

See Section 4, Principle 7: Learning

The philosophy behind prototyping is that you can learn faster by experimenting with ideas at an early stage. "Once new ideas begin to crystallise, they can be tried out fast, an approach that is alien to mainstream bureaucratic practice. Designers tend to favour rapid prototyping; learning fast by doing things rather than very detailed planning" says Geoff Mulgan of NESTA. Participants need to feel a sense of play: trying things out, welcoming failure as a way of learning, being curious for feedback on how things can be improved.

The Convergence stage is not easy; as a facilitator, you may sometimes need to take on an unpopular role and insist that participants make clear choices, even when difficult. If they don't, the group will become stuck at the final stage of Commitment. The end product of Convergence should be a range of clear options ready for decision making.

TOOL 43
Prototyping[24]

Prototyping allows you to make ideas tangible quickly and cheaply so that they can be tested and evaluated by others. Groups can build models, create storyboards, perform a role play, or make a diagram to show the idea to others. It doesn't need to be perfect. It just needs to help you answer questions about the idea.

60 minutes ✶✶✶✶✶

TOOL 44
Prioritising and Ranking

This tool will help you to select the most promising ideas or options when many have been generated. Ask everyone to agree on the names of the ideas, explain the rules (e.g. "we'll keep the best three"), and ask people to vote.

15-30 minutes ✶✶✶✶✶

TOOL 45
Comparing Proposals[25]

This tool is a simple matrix for weighing proposals from different perspectives. It captures alternative proposals developed by the group, and analyses the corresponding trade-offs. It will help the group understand that there are different options, and that there are no easy answers to complex issues.

60 minutes ✶✶✶✶✶

TOOL 46
Feedback from Stakeholders

If co-creation with certain stakeholders is difficult, you can still obtain feedback on ideas that the MSP is considering or developing. There are a number of ways of getting feedback including citizen juries, field testing, and feedback surveys (see Tool 54).

A couple of days to 3 weeks
✶✶✶✶✶

TOOL 47
Ritual Dissent [26]

This tool is designed to test and enhance proposals, stories, or ideas by subjecting them to ritualised dissent (challenge) or assent (positive alternatives). The tool enables presenters to get feedback in a safe environment and to review their proposals more critically.

90 minutes ✶✶✶✶✶

TOOL 48
Card Clustering

Use coloured cards for individuals to write ideas (one idea per card). These are shared and validated, and put up for all to see with similar ideas together in a cluster. Aim for consensus when moving cards around and naming clusters. Can be used at various stages.

60–90 minutes ✶✶✶✶✶

TOOL 49
Socratic Dialogue

This is a form of dialogue that uses universal questions to help a group discover what something is. It takes a question relevant to the MSP - such as "Can conflict be fruitful?" - and then facilitator and participants (5–15 people) push the dialogue forward through questioning using personal examples. Consensus is valued. Requires trust.

60–120 minutes ✶✶✶✶✶

TOOL 50
A Change of Scene

Before major decisions or breakthroughs are made, it can be useful to do something completely different. One way is to take people out of the meeting environment on excursions, field visits, or reflection walks. This refreshes the mind and gives people time to ponder the implications of decisions. Even a 20-minute walk in pairs can make a big difference to the productivity and collaborative capacity of a diverse group.

20 minutes to half a day
✶✶✶✶✶

TOOL 51
Silence

Don't underestimate the power of silence. Some of the best contributions may come from introverts who need a bit of time to collect their thoughts, based on their active listening. Ask people to spend 10 minutes with their reflection journals, and afterwards discuss their reflections with 1 or 2 other people. Or ask in plenary to hear from someone who has not spoken much.

10-30 minutes ✶✶✶✶✶

■ Individual: fairly simple   ■ Requires interaction: colleagues / partners   ■ Complex: needs preparation   ✶ Grades in difficulty

Commitment: Agreement on actions, and alignment and reflection

The main aim of the Commitment stage is to make decisions and agree upon actions. Tools for prioritising, ranking, and decision making can help to structure the decision making process, and avoid meetings ending in indecision or a stakeholder group hijacking the agenda to push their preferred solutions. Remember that participants also need to agree on ways to stay accountable to each other for implementing the actions.

Some meetings may be less structured and more explorative, and rely less on defining follow-up actions for their success. The purpose should still be clear enough for participants to know whether the meeting was successful. Use participatory evaluation tools to help.

It is not only clear decisions that make for a memorable, impactful meeting. Commitment also grows when people feel inspired and empowered to do something about the issue for which the MSP was created. If previous stages have been managed well, you won't need to give a pep talk at the end because participants will already be satisfied about what they have done together. But do make sure that there is a proper moment for closure. It can be appropriate to have a high-ranking person wrap up the meeting. But usually, we prefer to let the group members themselves talk about what the meeting has meant for them, how they see next steps taking place, and what they have learned. Providing space for these closing comments is the best way to build and sustain commitment.

TOOL 52

Set Decision Rules[27]

A decision rule is a mechanism that lets you know for sure when you have made a decision. In MSPs, the diversity of interests is large and consensus difficult, and not all decisions need unanimity. This tool will help you to distinguish which decisions need what type of procedure.

Main time investment is in preparation ★★★★★

TOOL 53

Make a Visual Theory of Change

This tool is used to visualise the process for the intended change. It answers the question: "How do we think change will happen in this MSP"? It can include the expected benchmarks or preconditions needed to reach long-term change.

2-3 hours ★★★★★

TOOL 54

Polls

If the group can't decide unanimously on a course of action, voting can be used. Methods include stickers (give everybody three stickers to allocate to their preferred options on the flipchart), raising hands (although people might influence each other), and using free online services like Shakespeak (live in the meeting, using your mobiles) or Surveymonkey (for polls and surveys outside a meeting).

Main time investment is in preparation ★★★★★

TOOL 55

Fish Bowl

A small group sits in a circle and discusses the topic while participants listen - or join in by moving their chair into the middle. Useful if the topic demands one conversation in a large group instead of breakouts. Evokes active listening.

45-90 minutes ★★★★★

TOOL 56

Reflection[28]

Commitment is enhanced if participants can reflect on the group's work and link it to their day-to-day work. Reflection exercises, both individually and in groups, can be used to make the insights stick. The CDI Reflection booklet has more than 40 tools.

15-45 minutes ★★★★★

TOOL 57

Synthesis

You can help participants remember insights and agreements by asking them to summarise these for themselves. Use one-minute elevator pitches, creating a drawing or poster, or choosing a metaphor, to help participants represent what the MSP means to them or how they see their own role.

15-60 minutes ★★★★★

TOOL 58

Option One-and-a-Half[29]

Instead of deciding between two solutions to a problem or situation, this tool helps you use the two solutions to develop a third. It can create agreement out of disagreement.

60 minutes ★★★★★

TOOL 59

Closing Circle

Instead of a dry evaluation exercise, end by allowing all participants to briefly share how they feel, or what they take home from this meeting, in one sentence - or if time is short, in one or two words only. This is more memorable than a summary from the facilitator or chair.

15-30 minutes ★★★★★

TOOL 60

Evaluation

Evaluating participants' feedback on a meeting is relevant for your own learning, and for accountability to a sponsor. We prefer to get feedback on 3-6 questions before people leave. Post-meeting questionnaires have a low response rate.

20-30 minutes ★★★★★

■ Individual: fairly simple   ■ Requires interaction: colleagues / partners   ■ Complex: needs preparation   ★ Grades in difficulty

7 MSPs IN ACTION

How do MSPs work in practice? Do you need a strong and charismatic leader to ensure success? What happens when there is a large power imbalance between stakeholders? Or when enthusiasm wanes, and the whole approach seems to be one long challenge? How does it feel to be involved in situations of misunderstanding and conflict? What can you learn?

By their nature, MSPs are extremely varied and are driven by people from different sectors, different walks of life, and with different styles of leadership. MSPs can be initiated by governments, the private sector, civil society organisations, knowledge institutions, or simply ordinary citizens concerned about an issue. It helps to have a strong and persistent initiator, but MSPs thrive when the initiator can make their concern a shared concern and create a core group that leads collaboratively.

See Section 4: Collaborative leadership and Section 5: Facilitation

This section brings you some stories from people who have experienced the ups and downs of working with multiple stakeholders. Each of them is a respected leader in his or her own field, but they all come from very different working backgrounds and have experience of very different MSPs. You will find stories from a civil society leader, a business network leader, a diplomat, two directors of a producer organisation, and a scientist. Together they will give you a diverse picture of the practice of facilitating MSPs as seen from the perspectives of different sectors and parts of the world.

MSPs IN ACTION

Be positive, be persistent, listen first: A civil society perspective

"You could consider my professional identity to be an MSP in itself: I started as a banker and became increasingly convinced that traditional banking services were not helping the poor in India. So I founded the NGO Sampark. Using my financial expertise and what I have learned from the realities of poor women in rural areas, we try to innovate financial services that help vulnerable people to gain direct control over and improve their lives. Through this work, I became increasingly involved with advising and collaborating with the public sector, which sets and implements policies. So I got to know the way the government and UN system work. And I have always worked as an academic as well, to reflect on my practical experience and contribute to the development of knowledge. I am happy with combining these roles, as long as I can link grassroots experience to wider policy discussions.

In 35 years of working with multiple stakeholders for rural development, I have learned that it boils down to four words: connect, listen, reflect, and express. Each of these four activities requires a different skill set. I had to learn that I needed to build my own capacity in some of these skills. The order of these four words is also important. It starts with connecting to other people's humanity – the name of the NGO I founded, Sampark, means 'to connect'. Only then are you able to listen to what others have to say, and only then will you be able to reflect back what you perceive and write about it. Whenever I switch the order, I am limiting my ability to influence the process effectively.

Recently, I was invited to join a Task Force on Poverty Alleviation for the State of Madhya Pradesh. This is a government-led MSP that tries to find ways to reduce the huge inequalities that exist in this state of 75 million inhabitants, which are causing extreme poverty and social unrest. I am the NGO representative on the task force. The five people on it combine a huge amount of experience in the public sector and international agencies. I brought in the perspective of putting first the people for whom the Task Force was created. Let me given an example. One of the ideas of the government is to introduce cash transfers as a way to replace the public distribution system, which is currently operated through fair price shops where poor people can

Dr Smita Premchander

Founder member and Honorary Chief Executive of the NGO Sampark (www.sampark.org Bangalore, India). Consultant to UN, donors, NGOs and research institutes. Member of Task Force on Poverty Eradication of the State of Madhya Pradesh, India. Visiting professor at the Indian Institute of Management (Ahmedabad), CDI Wageningen UR, and other universities in Asia, Europe and America

access rice, wheat, sugar, and kerosene through a government ration card. In theory, the benefits of switching to cash transfers are many: it is efficient and less prone to corruption. But when I sat down with 50 villagers to discuss their views, the women spoke out strongly against cash transfers. 'Cash will go to alcohol'. I asked the men if they agreed with this view. One man said: 'Yes, in fact we do not act responsibly to our families. With one slap I can get as much money as I need from my wife. If you want the children to have food for a month, better give grain to the women'. My conclusion is that it is too early for cash transfers. I brought these voices from the field back to my Task Force, where they are taken on board in the discussion. I am aware that I will need to compromise in these discussions at some point. I will also surely keep on listening to arguments put forward by supporters and opponents of cash transfers. In some areas of Madhya Pradesh, 80% of the people are poor by any standard. We need a variety of approaches (basic services, skill development, enterprise development) to start tackling this, and I am hopeful because the government recognises the need to involve all sectors in this endeavour.

I have seen as many MSPs fail as I have seen succeed. If stakeholders are not willing to give up their ways, it will fail. I still regret how an MSP around a watershed project ended badly. Some government and development bank staff wanted 10% of the project value as a bribe. Our NGO refused as it is against our values. The villagers wanted to get the 90% and nevertheless urged us to continue. At that time, we had more power than the villagers and we stuck to our 'no'. As a result, the bank pulled out. People interpreted our action to mean that we did not help them to access government resources well, and the project closed after one or two years. In hindsight, I believe we stood too much on our values. Perhaps more dialogue could have opened new solutions that respected our values, as well as the villagers' needs. But perhaps it was bound to fail anyway, because if we had allowed them to take the money, our values would have been compromised, and our NGO would not have commanded the respect it has in the community today. In any case, we realised the importance of carefully organising an MSP. The MSP design determines whether we have the right conversations with stakeholders.

I have learned that you need to be positive in MSPs. You have to believe in dialogue, even if some government staff think that all NGOs are crooks. I have also learned to be realistic about the different agendas that each stakeholder brings to the table. We have different worldviews and political preferences, and an MSP is not necessarily going to smooth these out. But we can develop new solutions together. Another lesson I learned is about the management of expectations. When representatives of stakeholder groups join an MSP, they carry huge expectations from their constituents. This makes negotiations very hard. Finally, I learned that as an NGO it is better to be lean and smart than to be large when engaging in MSP debates. It requires a certain agility and people-orientation that smaller NGOs seem to be better at."

Trust, patience and letting go: A business platform perspective

"I have spent my whole career working on corporate social responsibility and looking at what companies need to do in order to set and achieve sustainability goals. Two decades ago, I was already working on the business case for the actions that companies could take. I have come a long way since and now see that what a company needs to do actually depends on the whole system in which they operate. So individual actions are not enough. It has become very clear to me that we need honest brokers and effective platforms that bring stakeholders together to create system-wide change.

For me, having first worked with Syngenta on Grow Africa, the opportunity to help set up Grow Asia as an innovative multi-stakeholder platform was very appealing. With the backing of ASEAN governments, leading businesses, and civil society, and building on ongoing partnerships in Vietnam, Indonesia, and Myanmar, Grow Asia has much potential to help drive sustainable agriculture across the region.

The way I think about my role is bringing people to the same table and creating an environment of trust where there can be genuine conversations about opportunities to tackle common issues. In all this, fostering trust is the key ingredient and a very big part of what I do.

The legitimacy of the platform is also important. We have the backing of the World Economic Forum, which enables us to convene stakeholders at the highest level and bring on board Ministers of Agriculture, CEOs, and other leaders. This leader level engagement is important to ensure organisational commitment and the buy-in needed to drive system-wide change.

What I have learned about multi-stakeholder platforms is that you shouldn't try to control them too much. You can guide it in certain directions, and then you have to give the space for all stakeholders to own it themselves and decide where they want it to go. My job is to create the supportive structures and guiding principles that help to keep all the stakeholders engaged and trust the process.

Kavita Prakash-Mani

Executive Director of Grow Asia[1] - a multi-stakeholder partnership initiated by business through the World Economic Forum to help drive sustainable agriculture in the ASEAN region. It aims to reach 10 million small-scale farmers and enable a 20% increase in yields, profits, and environmental sustainability.

A lot of the mistrust between NGOs, government, and business comes from the historic adversarial and campaign-oriented approaches by NGOs. Of course, these were very helpful in getting issues on the agenda and creating a business case for action. But now that there is much more recognition of the seriousness of sustainability issues, there is also recognition about the need to work together on finding solutions as we see in the value chain projects catalysed by Grow Asia, where all the stakeholders work together to create shared value for the farmers and all the players in the value chain. I think trust is about people seeing that others are genuinely interested in finding common solutions by working together. There will always be vested interests. But we have to create win-win solutions that will enable the greater good to be found as well as individual interests to be met.

For stakeholders to engage, they need a deep trust in the individuals and organisations that convene such platforms. We lose our partners if they don't trust Grow Asia or they don't trust me. The honest broker role in the middle is key in holding everyone equally to account and ensuring that the agenda is not dominated (or perceived to be dominated) by the vested interests of particular groups. Individuals do make a difference. As a key representative of the platform, I feel that this trust is gained when stakeholders see that I have a very clear purpose in working for their collective interests. The platform and I stand for new models of agricultural development, rural economic growth, and environmental sustainability that will be in everyone's interests. My passion for the work of the platform and an open and honest personal agenda is also an important aspect in gaining buy-in from stakeholders.

Despite the growing attention being paid to multi-stakeholder platforms, we are all still on a steep learning curve. I don't think there are any examples that have really sorted it out completely with success at multiple levels. But we have seen significant traction with initiatives such as the Round Table on Sustainable Palm Oil, the World Cocoa Foundation, Grow Africa, or the Materials Sustainability Index initiated by Nike. All these initiatives are bringing businesses together in a pre-competitive space to tackle sustainability issues.

An enormous challenge for me in supporting the Grow Asia Partnership is to find the right balance of using my convening role to drive the agenda forward, while at the same time making everyone feel empowered to be part of the decision making. If we don't show results and move quickly enough, stakeholders will not consider it worthwhile; on the other hand, if we go too fast, stakeholders will feel left out. We must have the patience to let everyone walk the journey. It is really about finding the sweet spot between action, speed, and taking people along.

In taking on the convening role, we need to make sure we don't overload people's lives with these partnerships. Stakeholders have many roles and responsibilities; we can't assume that what we do is necessarily the most important thing for them."

To be effective in my facilitation and brokering role, I have learned that I need passion, patience, and acceptance that we are all on a journey. What you think is the right way of doing is not necessarily the right way, or the only right way, of doing it. You need to constantly learn and re-evaluate as you move forward, and give people the space that they need. There are a lot of good ideas out there that just need to be nurtured.

The skills and capabilities of people supporting multi-stakeholder partnerships are really important. It can be a lonely role as you try to hold everything together, and at the end of the day, you feel a lot of responsibility. Opportunities for guidance, sharing, and learning with others in the same boat are really needed."

Finally, they shook hands: A public sector perspective

"When I became the new Dutch Ambassador to Nigeria in 2009, I wanted to see the problem with my own eyes. I knew that the Niger Delta was heavily polluted due to oil spills after decades of oil exploitation by companies such as Shell.[2] But when I stood face-to-face with people who had lost their livelihoods, and saw the conditions of their land and creeks, I was shocked. Thick layers of oil had covered parts of the land and water; sometimes it had been there for years. Bodo, a community of 50,000 people, is one example of oil winning gone completely awry after the oil pipeline crossing Bodo leaked oil twice in 2008.

What was also shocking was the level of distrust between all the parties involved. High-profile lawsuits, international advocacy by environmental NGOs, intimidation at the local level, and a passive response from the relevant authorities had resulted in a situation where nothing was happening. It seemed a hopeless case. Yet, now, six years later, there is a €70 million settlement with Shell, a proper clean-up operation being implemented, and a dialogue structure where all stakeholders talk to each other.

But let me go back to my early days in Nigeria. Citizen protests against the oil industry had been intense in the nineties, under the leadership of Nigerian writer Ken Saro-Wiwa. Environmental NGOs had rallied for years blaming Shell

Bert Ronhaar

Former Ambassador of the Kingdom of the Netherlands to Nigeria. Special Envoy of The Netherlands to Nigeria for the conflict over pollution in Ogoniland in the Niger Delta.

and other companies for not cleaning up dozens of oil spills. The companies were faced with huge dilemmas: they knew that oil spills took place under their guard, but at the same time, there was much vandalism by local people tapping illegal oil from the pipes and causing pollution by refining the crude oil in an uncontrolled manner. The Joint Inspection Visits that Shell conducted to document new spill incidents were criticized by Amnesty International for containing wrong information. The Government of Nigeria concluded that it was the company's responsibility to clean up, and left it at that. The UN produced an independent environmental assessment on the oil spills in Ogoniland in 2011, so there was a solid knowledge base.

The Dutch Embassy has a long track record in balancing the interests of different stakeholders. We have supported many human rights initiatives over the years in Nigeria and built up strong relationships with civil society. But of course, we also represent the interests of Shell, which after all is a Dutch–British company. In the Netherlands, protest against Shell was growing and questions were asked in parliament about the Niger Delta. So it quickly became a top priority for me to deal with this conflict. I thought, "It's a very difficult problem, but not one that can't be solved". We had a partner network that was already involved, and we were working together with the British and French Embassies, so we became a natural party to convene stakeholders. People warned me that this conflict was 'too hot to handle' and that I couldn't do anything to solve it during my tenure as ambassador. But I am a practical person by nature, and I thought, "Let's try. If I don't do it, who else can play this neutral role towards all stakeholders?"

At the end of 2012, I decided to link up with one of our partners, NACGOND, a constructive coalition of eighteen environmental NGOs. Together with their chairman, Inemo Samiama, we started to talk around. An important lesson I learned: if you are an outsider wanting to mediate in a conflict, always work together with a neutral local party who can provide cultural insider's knowledge. We decided to focus on the Bodo community: a heavily polluted area and politically very divided. If we could have a successful dialogue in Bodo, we could succeed anywhere in Nigeria. Bodo was a no-go area for Shell officials because of the level of anger of the community, as well as the risk of kidnapping. A retired Dutch priest who had ministered in the area for many years offered to come with us, and through his networks, we were received warmly. I was the first ambassador to go and stand there with my feet in the oil. I could understand the impasse: people had constructed enemy images against Shell that were historically justified.

By April 2013, we had spoken to all the stakeholders: the Federal State, the State, the Shell Petroleum Development Company, top management and executive staff, contractors, local leaders, NGOs, and of course the citizens of Bodo. Both the villagers and Shell said: "If you believe it can work, we'll give it a try". Gradually it seemed there was consensus about four things, which I called the 'poles in the ground':
1. Cleaning up is Shell's responsibility.
2. The community needs to do something against illegal oil refineries.

3. The clean-up needs to be implemented by reputed international contractors, not local contractors (due to conflicts of interest of the latter).
4. Independent experts should supervise the implementation of the clean-up to ensure it is done to international standards.

We thought this gave a sufficient basis to organise a first meeting. But the meeting was delayed for four months because of a huge disagreement within the Bodo community on who could represent them. A traditional leader insisted: "If my own sub-contractors can't participate, there won't be a deal". We created a pre-mediation committee, consisting of local religious leaders, NACGOND, and citizens not in dispute, to deal with the deadlock. We insisted that contractors or political parties were not welcome, as this process was not suitable for those with a direct interest. I joined these meetings to support Inemo and to remind everybody about these 'poles in the ground'. These were tough and emotional meetings with 40 people. We only made progress when we kicked out all the lawyers after half a day. People did not mix; they physically sat on different sides of the room.

The first stakeholder meeting in summer 2013 brought three opposing sides together: Shell, the Bodo community, and the environmental NGOs. Lawyers came in to threaten with a court case. I was able to convince them to put this on hold, pending this dialogue process. We engaged a professional mediator from the Centre for Humanitarian Dialogue in Geneva who trained stakeholders and assisted in negotiating. The outcome was that three working groups were formed to look at the technical aspects of the clean-up, pipeline integrity, and socio-economist development. Shell made €7 million available for this as a sign of goodwill. We also invited the new reconciliation commission, led by Catholic priests, to give a report on their efforts to resolve the conflict in Bodo. This was a way to bring the voices of people on the ground into the discussion, a reality check.

After my retirement in 2014, the Minister asked if I would stay on as a Special Envoy to facilitate this ongoing dialogue. Of course, I obliged, as we were so close to a resolution. We were thankful to experience a milestone in 2015, which you will have seen in the media:[3] Shell settled with Bodo for €70 million of compensation. The largest part is to be paid directly into the personal bank accounts of 15,600 fishermen and farmers, amounting to €2,800 per claimant. The remainder has been put in a community development fund where it serves to improve education, health, and economic development in Bodo. The clean-up is ready to start. It will still take a long time before Bodo is normalized, I expect it to be ten to twenty years before the ecosystem is clean again.

Many people congratulate me on this result. I have to correct them: the stakeholder leaders themselves stepped over their shadows and made this happen. I don't think the Dutch government necessarily needs to take a leading role for other polluted areas in the Niger Delta. My co-chair Inemo Samiamo or NACGOND could play that role very well."

It's never a solo flight: A producer organisation's perspective

"Sugarcane is a hardy crop that is key to the livelihoods of our 23,000 members: all growers of sugarcane in South Africa. Although it is hardy, it is also delicate, because once harvested, the cane needs to be processed immediately to get the best amount and quality of sugar. If you wait too long, the value of the harvest decreases dramatically. That is the reason behind the strong dependency of all players in the sugar value chain. Growers rely on the transporters and sugar mills and vice versa. Our collective success depends on our ability to make it work, together.

CANEGROWERS realised that many problems in the sugar industry were not necessarily because of a lack of technical knowledge – we have capable research institutes and support services. It is the social facilitation aspect that was missing. For example, our local grower committees were not equipped to deal with the conflicts arising between growers, millers, and transporters. And at a higher level, many small-scale growers were not really involved in the industry decisions that affected them. As our mission is to lead, protect, communicate, and serve the interests of sugarcane growers, we realised we needed to build our own capacity to facilitate better interaction between all the actors in the sugar value chain.

You should know that sugar production and processing in South Africa is a mature industry, but it is undergoing huge changes as a result of several factors. First, we are part of post-apartheid South Africa and have to deal with the inequalities and social unrest that are part of our journey in this day and age. People are in need of jobs, and people who were once dispossessed are having their land returned to them. Recently, a large sugarcane farm was transferred to a community of about 8,500 individuals who were part of a claimant group – you can imagine the challenges of getting this organised. To put this into perspective, 38% of the sugarcane area in South Africa is currently the subject of land claims by communities who have come forward saying "We want our land back". Second, we all worry about the sustainability of the sugarcane industry. We have been facing droughts beyond the normal weather variability for the last decade, and have to conclude that it is because of climate change. Worldwide, including in South Africa, sugar industries are facing declining margins between returns and the cost of production, due to a long-

Dr Kathy Hurly
Director, Regional Services of CANEGROWERS,
South Africa www.sacanegrowers.co.za

Thandokwakhe Sibiya
Director, Grower Sustainability of
CANEGROWERS, South Africa

term downward trend in the price of sugar. People doubt whether sugarcane can continue to provide a sustainable income in South Africa.

We get involved in facilitating MSPs at several levels in the sugar sector: from interactions between small-scale growers and their local stakeholders, to high-level industry decision-making. In both situations, we benefit from the MSP tools we have been trained in. Let us give two examples.

In Noodsberg, our grower support officers have been helping groups of growers to take joint decisions. There was a conflict between several small-scale cooperatives about how to move forward with their business. The growers even threatened to burn their cane so that the mill would not get anything. In an emergency meeting, the growers met with the milling company and the bank.

See Section 6, Tool 3

We know that these meetings can get quite violent, so we decided to facilitate carefully. We asked everybody to draw rich pictures of the current situation. This helped to disentangle the problem so that people could understand and discuss it, and together with the bank, we solved the conflict. The local association of cooperatives found a way to restructure their businesses. They managed to repay their debt to the bank after our intervention. The business is now stable.

We have also used these types of tools in higher-level policy discussions. Of course, we adapt them based on the objective and the people who are present. We like visualisation tools, but we also know that some more highly educated people don't see this as a professional way of working. We disagree, but there are many other tools that we can use to help stakeholders have better conversations and make better decisions. One example: our industry is organised in 'vertical slices', decentralised structures comprising particular mills, their supplier growers, and downstream processing. Each vertical slice makes its own plan together with the three main types of canegrowers: large-scale growers, small-scale growers, and land reform growers. There are huge power imbalances between these growers and the mills, and between the growers themselves. Recently we sat down with grower groups in Mpumalanga Province, Makhatini Flats, and the Tongaat Hulett Grower Forum, which is composed of grower leaders who supply to four Tongaat Hullet sugar mills in KwaZulu-Natal north coast. We helped these growers to formulate strategies for negotiating on value adding opportunities with the millers in their vertical slices. Our challenge was to ensure that the weakest voices could contribute effectively in this process. The usual mindset in the industry is that educated people do all the talking and assume that their ideas for the industry are the most important. But in fact, many growers have good ideas too, even if they don't appreciate all the complexities of the policies governing the industry. We see it as one of our tasks to help our growers learn so that they can prepare themselves for these discussions in the vertical slice. It can take time to come to an informed joint decision, but eventually a good buy-in can be achieved from everybody involved. This is essential because, as we know from the past, a lack of buy-in upfront leads to conflict and deadlock later on during implementation.

What we have learned? Many things.

"WE TAKE THE
TIME TO ALIGN
DIFFERENT
STAKEHOLDERS,
BUILD THEIR
CAPACITY, AND
ORGANISE
PROCESSES AND
PLATFORMS
WHERE PEOPLE
CAN GIVE INPUT
AND FEEL
CONNECTED"

Let's start with patience. We have often been in situations where other stakeholders thought that we were wasting time. But now we think they realise our value: we take the time to align different stakeholders, build their capacity, and organise processes and platforms where people can give input and feel connected to a larger discussion about the future of the industry. Increasingly we work in partnership with other industry stakeholders. We discuss upfront what we can do, what we expect from each other, how we see each other's roles.

We have also learned to trust the process to take its course. This is difficult if you come from a positivist scientific mind-set, as both of us have. Sometimes we already think we know the best solution for a problem and could solve it quickly. Then we need our patience to see the process out, making sure that everybody stays on board.

And we learned to expect surprises. MSPs never go according to a pre-defined plan. We see people go into a panic-mode when things don't go according to plan. But by now we know that it is never straight from A to B: along the way there will be curve balls. This doesn't mean that your process is failing. It simply calls upon you to constantly assess what's happening, and adjust your tools and methods accordingly.

Finally: work with someone. Look out for people who can mentor you, who have access to different networks, who can give you feedback. It's never a solo flight."

Listen first, then learn together: A science perspective

"As a scientist, I have always been fascinated by the natural world: how it supports life on this planet, and how we humans can use it to feed ourselves. For most of my career, I have studied food crops, in particular in Africa. My current work focuses on putting nitrogen fixation to work for smallholder farmers in Africa growing legume crops such as climbing bean, common bean, soybean, and groundnut. These crops also happen to be rich in protein and minerals and relatively easy to produce, which makes them very efficient for feeding the planet's growing population in an environmentally sustainable way.

My role as a scientist is to produce new knowledge and innovations. But my ambition is also to make sure that science is relevant – that it contributes to solving real world problems. And gradually I have learned that, in order for new insights to emerge, we as scientists must collaborate and interact, first of all with scientists of other disciplines. You will have noticed that I do quite technical research on soils, crops, and farm production systems. By working with farmers in Africa, I quickly found out that technical solutions are not the only solutions required. There is also a human and social side to farming systems and crop production. I could give detailed recommendations to farmers on which legume crop would give the best yields and keep their soil healthy, but I realised that their livelihoods also depended on the security of land ownership, on economic opportunities created for youth in or outside agriculture, and gender issues, to name but a few. So I started to collaborate within our university with technical and social scientists. Let me describe this experience, as it gave me much insight into successful collaboration in partnerships.

I led an interdisciplinary core group of scientists from different disciplines around the theme of 'Competing Claims on Natural Resources'. We tried to understand what happens when different people or stakeholders have different, competing claims on a natural resource (a wildlife park, a river, a plot of land). Every few weeks we would meet for a lunch discussion, and we were getting nowhere. Everybody defended their own stance, was keen to show how important their science was, and all talked in their own specialist jargon. So I had to set one new ground rule: if we intervene, we have to come with a positive contribution. This had immediate effect. People simplified their language, and took better care to communicate properly. What kept this group together was a common wish and will to learn. It led to us putting 'negotiation' central in a framework for engagement we called the DEED Cycle (Describe, Explain, Explore, Design).[4] This helped us to map out what we were doing as researchers, and in which order we should organise our research. It is a dynamic action research framework, not a fixed model. It allowed all of us to first get a grounded understanding of competing claims, to develop scenarios and possible futures, and from there design actions. Together with other stakeholders like park rangers, local community leaders, environmental NGOs like WWF, and development NGOs like Caritas, we applied it in many situations in Africa, such as national parks, forest reserves, and wetlands. We jointly supervised 15 PhD students, started a course[5] for mid-career professionals with CDI, and published[6] widely on competing claims. The concept of 'competing claims' now stands on its own and has become embedded in the policy of the Dutch government. And there is still residual work going on in South Africa and Zimbabwe. If I look back, the initial investment we needed to make to

Professor Ken Giller

Professor of Plant Production Systems, Wageningen University. Project leader of N2Africa (Putting Nitrogen Fixation to Work for Smallholder Farmers in Africa: www.n2africa.org) funded by the Bill & Melinda Gates Foundation

understand each other as scientists, paid off very well. Our struggles helped us to communicate better with external stakeholders in later stages of the action research.

Let me give a second example of how I operate in MSPs as a scientist. Some years ago, the Bill & Melinda Gates Foundation approached me with this question: "What do you know about legume crops and nitrogen fixation that we can put into action now to help smallholders in Africa to increase their yields?" Of course I had some ideas, but we started by proposing consultations with our African colleagues. What do we know about legume crops? How can we use them to intensify production and to diversify the production system of farmers in Africa? We came up with N2Africa (www.N2Africa.org), a five-year programme led by Wageningen University together with the International Institute of Tropical Agriculture (IITA) and the International Livestock Research Institute (ILRI). We have many partners in DR Congo, Ghana, Ethiopia, Kenya, Mozambique, Malawi, Nigeria, Rwanda, Tanzania, Uganda, and Zimbabwe (Tier 1 countries).

What is interesting about this programme is how we learn. We start with a real problem, and in each country scale up to work with 30,000–50,000 farmers. We deliberately work at a large scale – it pushes us to learn faster and to engage with other actors in the value chain beyond the farm gate. We avoid doing research with only one group or area, or doing only small pilots. If we develop a new insight, we can immediately back it up with data from a large group of collaborating farmers.

The role of a researcher in facilitating such a massive collaboration is very different from regular academic tasks. I had to learn how to perform some of these roles on the job, and I am still learning. My role in this MSP has three elements. First, to document what happens and what we learn from it – this comes naturally to me as a researcher. Second, to discuss with a wide range of stakeholders including farmers, NGOs, extension agents, and companies. I don't lecture, but experimenting farmers and others in the value chain find it helpful to know how legumes can contribute by fixing nitrogen from the atmosphere. Likewise, I benefit from their experience. Third, I communicate with governments and with the Bill & Melinda Gates Foundation in Seattle. I try to understand their policies and can make suggestions to align or overhaul policies to create more impact.

What I learned from driving this type of MSP process is that it is humbling. Many things go on outside our sphere of influence – we are not the only ones trying to change things. I also learned the value of listening to others, and being able to receive and give feedback. Only by investing in communication can stakeholders align themselves to a common goal. Finally, one benefit of working with such a diverse group of partners is that you can seek advice. I can count on the expertise and networks of others, just by sharing my concern and asking for help."

8 ADDITIONAL RESOURCES

This section contains some additional resources, both for rapid reference and to help you deepen your understanding of MSPs. It also provides more detail on the wide range of academic and practice-based knowledge that lies behind this guide and on the sources of our inspiration. The first part looks briefly at the theoretical concepts that underlie our practice of facilitating MSPs and points you toward the main researchers involved in their development. This is followed by a list of recommended texts on the main topics of this guide. Finally, we list a number of websites that have useful material for the design and facilitation of MSPs.

Five underlying concepts

We identify five different concepts as providing the basic foundation for the overarching idea of MSPs, and also the theoretical justification for the systemic, participatory, and learning-oriented approach of this guide. We cannot do justice to the full breadth of the theory underlying these concepts within this brief section. Instead, we give a brief summary and refer you for deeper understanding to the main authors who have inspired our thoughts.

Concept 1: Governance

As mentioned in Section 1, governance means the way in which people (a local group, a business, a country, the global community) make collective decisions and coordinate action to serve their common interests. Societies have many different mechanisms of governance; government (the state) is just one form. Both businesses and NGOs have governance structures and communities often have informal governance mechanisms. A whole network of governance mechanisms exists in the government, private, and civil society sectors, from the local to the global scale.

In the modern world, the nation state remains the dominant governance structure, with a trend towards most states at least claiming to be democratic. However, globalisation means the decision-making power of the state is constrained. National governments have to contend internationally with issues that cross national boundaries, such as global market forces, climate change, disease, and water resource management. Domestically, governments struggle to balance short-term politics with longer-term social and environmental concerns and intergenerational interests. In addition, many countries still lack the basics of transparency and accountability that underpin effective governance.

These difficulties come at a historical point in time when globalisation, with its associated ecological, economic, and social issues, makes effective governance more critical for the future of humankind than ever before. It is in this context that business, NGOs, and government often turn to MSP-type approaches as a mechanism for working around the constraints of existing governance mechanisms.

Numerous authors have explored the dilemmas of governance in the modern world and many propose that the way forward is to deepen democracy, making it more participatory, with greater engagement of citizens and stakeholder groups in decision making. Ulrich Beck,[1] for example, talks of a 'risk society', the need for a 'reinvention of politics', and the forms of 'sub-politics' that emerge when governance mechanisms fail. Claus Offe[2] explores the enormous challenges of coordination for the nation state, while David Held,[3] John Dryzek,[4] and Anthony Giddens[5] all offer perspectives on what new and more effective forms of governance might be like. Much of the thinking on participatory and interactive forms of governance has its theoretical foundations in the work of the sociologist Jürgen Habermas,[5] who argued the importance of 'communicative rationality' for societies to cope with complex and ethically challenging problems. MSPs are very much oriented towards strengthening this type of communicative rationality.

The theoretical foundations of governance are also linked to the concept of good governance. The United Nations Development Programme (UNDP), for example, claims that good governance should be consensus-oriented, participatory, accountable, transparent, responsive, efficient and effective, and equitable and inclusive, while following the rule of law. MSPs contribute in many ways to these principles and should also uphold them.

It is beyond the scope of this guide to explore the wider ideas about governance in detail. But it is important that those who facilitate MSPs, and especially those who train others in MSP approaches, are aware of the wider governance context in which the practice of MSPs sits.

Concept 2: Complexity and resilience

Most MSPs try to create change in a complex system. In order to understand which change strategies may work, it is essential to understand how complex adaptive systems operate and respond. These types of system have been discussed briefly in Section 4 under Principle 1. Typically, a complex system has the following features:

· it involves large numbers of interacting elements;
· the interactions are nonlinear, and minor changes can have disproportionately major consequences; and
· the system is dynamic, which means solutions cannot be imposed on it, but instead arise from the circumstances. This is frequently referred to as emergence.

Some of the methods proposed in this guide are based on interdisciplinary research into complex adaptive systems, which brings together the best knowledge on ecology, systems theory, social sciences, and management studies.

In addition to research into the nature of complex adaptive systems, much work has been done into resilience – that is, into understanding why certain systems are particularly good at bouncing back after disruptions (e.g., Holling[7] 2002). Resilient social, ecological, or economic systems have the capacity to cope with disturbances and to recover in a way that maintains their core functions and identity. They can learn from and adapt to changing conditions. The figure shows the classic adaptive cycle that lies at the heart of resilience thinking. It focuses on the balance between continuity and change – a continuous cycle of release, reorganisation, exploitation, and conservation that characterises all resilient living systems.

The work of Snowden[8] is very helpful for learning how to deal with management challenges in complex adaptive systems. If you want to see what complexity thinking has to offer for the field of development assistance, Ramalingam[9] is a must. Zolli[10] and Westley[11] shed light on the factors that promote resilience in systems, people, and communities. Harford[12] explores success and failure in systems change in his book Adapt. For a deeper look at economics and systems theory, Eric Beinhocker[13] is an excellent read.

Concept 3: Cognition

When trying to create change in a complex system, we also have to take into account human cognition – that is, the way we perceive, process, and mentally respond to information. Cognition provides the basis for how people make decisions, form judgements about others, and act – and for the fact that people may act very differently to the way that they say (or think) that they do. Advances in psychology and cognitive science give us clues about what can make collaboration in MSPs successful.

Two lines of academic thinking have influenced our choices for this guide: the work of Nobel laureate Daniel Kahneman[14] and approaches related to behavioural economics.[15]

Kahneman stresses that the way our brain works leads us to make decisions that are not necessarily logical, even though we think that they are. He divides the brain into two agents, called System 1 and System 2, which produce fast and slow thinking, respectively. Both systems are active when we are awake, and generally work together well. System 1 is fast in recognising complex patterns – 'quick and dirty', intuitive, and effortless (e.g., driving a car on an empty road) – while System 2 is careful, analytical, and slow (e.g., telling somebody your telephone number). We tend to believe that our own thinking is guided by System 2, but in reality, much of the way we filter information, make decisions, and assess risks is informed by System 1 type routine judgements – which can lead to bias, error, and prejudiced decisions. In MSPs, we tend to assume that the stakeholders (and we ourselves) are making rational choices – but often they (and we) are not, or only to a limited extent. This can harm the decision-making process and the willingness to collaborate.

However, it is also important to recognise the benefits of System 1 decision-making, and that this kind of fast-track categorising and response is based on a large part on appropriate information and heuristics. Thus, it can be very useful, even when it is to some extent stereotypical. For example, when noticing that a number of women at a conference are wearing headscarves, we may 'intuitively' check rapidly that both juice and alcoholic drinks are being offered to all. The assumption that these women (and their male counterparts) are probably Muslim is indeed a stereotypical reaction, but it is also respectful to recognise that a group may have particular dietary requirements.

According to Kahneman, the best we can do to prevent the inappropriate use of short-cut thinking is a compromise: learn to recognise situations in which mistakes are likely and try harder to avoid significant mistakes when the stakes are high. We should also cultivate awareness of our assumptions, biases, and stereotypes and work with them when we can, as described by Enayati;[16] this includes in MSPs.

Another insight that has gained in relevance comes from behavioural economics. There is increasing agreement across the behavioural sciences that our behaviour is significantly influenced by factors associated with the context or situation in which we find ourselves. The UK Government's MINDSPACE framework[17] illustrates this approach. It draws heavily on work by behavioural economists[18] to describe nine major influences (Messenger, Incentives, Norms, Defaults, Salience, Priming, Affect, Commitments, Ego) that can be used to help understand, and identify ways to influence, individual behaviour. Behavioural economics suggests that instead of forcing people to do or not do something, policy makers should nudge people in the preferred direction. As the World Development Report[19] summarises: we think automatically (using mental shortcuts); we think socially (relying on social networks and norms); and we think with mental models (given to us by society and history). This offers challenges, but also creates opportunities for influencing the behaviour of stakeholders and their constituencies in our MSPs.

Concept 4: Innovation

Innovation is the holy grail of many MSPs: we know we need new solutions to deal with a challenge, but where do good ideas come from? What types of ecosystem are required to make innovation happen? How can we help innovations to have impact at scale? Several fields of inquiry have made useful contributions to our understanding of innovation: socio-technical transition theory, transition management, and innovation studies. A central idea in innovation systems is that these are nested wholes, embedded within each other.

We have found the work of Geels and Schot[20] helpful for understanding how novel ideas might lead to large-scale change. They propose three levels: niches (where radical novelties are just emerging, often unstable and at the fringe), patchworks of regimes (describing the current mainstream routines and rules – e.g., how we meet our food and water needs), and landscapes (changes in the wider environment/socio-cultural shifts over time). This model clarifies how transitions towards sustainability happen, and what route an innovation needs to take before becoming embedded in, and changing, dominant regimes and landscapes.

The following all provide useful insights if you want to learn more about transition and innovation. A recent contribution by Blok[21] comes from the area of responsible research and innovation, and looks at the ethical dimensions of, for example, new technological innovations. If you want to learn more about transition studies, which looks at how societies can shift towards more sustainability and equitability, consider the work of Jan Rotmans.[22] Finally, in recent years, we have learned more about the dynamics of agricultural innovation systems, including the roles of brokers and entrepreneurs in these systems.[23]

Concept 5: Partnerships

Academic interest in stakeholder engagement, (cross-sector) partnerships, and collaboration has been on the rise for the last three decades or more. Major contributions have come from business schools and public policy studies. The initial studies focused on collaboration between two partners from two different sectors – for example a business and an NGO, or government and a business. This resulted in useful classification models by Austin[24] of partnerships described as philanthropic, transactional, integrative, and transformative. Philanthropic and transactional partnerships involve companies giving money or services to an NGO, while integrative and transformative partnerships involve two partners creating new value that did not exist previously. Other studies have offered insights into what makes inter-organisational collaboration successful – for example, those by Gray[25] and Glasbergen.[26]

More recent studies have focused on partnerships, alliances, and networks that involve multiple actors or stakeholders. Their aim is often not simply to create value for the participants; rather they have greater ambitions, such as changing whole ecosystems or, as described by Waddell,[27] 'organising the field to advance a change agenda'. Examples include global multi-stakeholder initiatives such as the Roundtable for Sustainable Palm Oil or the Global Reporting Initiative. These illustrate the creation of new structures for collaborative governance, often transcending nation states.

A convergence appears to be taking place between different sectors, such as government, the private sector, civil society, research, and citizens. Most stakeholders realise that they can only achieve their goals if they work together with others, and they are developing their capability for this. Termeer and her co-authors[28] describe four governance capabilities that are essential for dealing with 'wicked problems'[29] (problems that hard to solve because they are ill-defined, ambiguous, and contested, and also feature multi-layered interdependencies and complex social dynamics): (a) reflexivity, or the capability to deal with multiple frames; (b) resilience, or the capability to adjust actions to uncertain changes; (c) responsiveness, or the capability to respond to changing agendas and expectations; (d) revitalisation, or the capability to unblock stagnation. These capabilities form the basis for achieving small wins in MSPs dealing with wicked problems. We also see an increase in critical reflections on the effectiveness of development or value chain partnerships, such as the study of Bitzer and Glasbergen.[30]

Recommended reading

There are a number of good books and other sources available that you can read or refer to if you want to deepen your understanding of MSPs and the concepts that underlie them. We have put together a list of the books (and one or two articles) that we think you will find most useful for each of the main topics in this guide: MSPs in general (Sections 1 and 2), process design and facilitation (Sections 3 and 5), and the seven principles described in Section 4. In each case, we have selected one book as top reading, suggested a few additional books (or articles) that would also be very useful, and given a classic publication for the topic. The publication details are in the reference list.

MSPs IN GENERAL

Top reading: **This book, of course!**

Also consider: **Barbara Gray and Jenne P. Sites** (2013) Sustainability through Partnerships: Capitalizing on Collaboration. Retrieved from: nbs.net/knowledge

Pieter Glasbergen, Frank Biermann, and Arthur Mol (eds.) (2007) Partnerships, Governance and Sustainable development: Reflections on Theory and Practice. http://tinyurl.com/nkbslk3

John Kania, Mark Kramer, and others (2011–2015) A series of articles on collective impact for Stanford Social Innovation Review: www.ssireview.org/articles/entry/collective_impact

Classic publication: **Minu Hemmati** (2002) Multi-Stakeholder Processes for Governance and Sustainability: Beyond Deadlock and Conflict.

PROCESS DESIGN AND FACILITATION

Top reading: **Sam Kaner, Lenny Lind, Catherine Toldi, Sarah Fisk, and Duane Berger** (2014, third edition) Facilitator's Guide to Participatory Decision-Making.

Also consider: **Noah Rimland Flower and Anna Muoio** (2014) GATHER: The Art and Science of Effective Convening. http://tinyurl.com/oddrp4k

Ros Tennyson (2005) The brokering guidebook: navigating partnerships for sustainable development http://tinyurl.com/pw5bm6s

Classic publication: **Jules Pretty, Irene Guijt, Ian Scoones, and John Thompson** (1995) Participatory Learning and Action: A Trainer's Guide. http://pubs.iied.org/6021IIED.html

PRINCIPLE 1: Embrace systemic change

Top reading: **Frances Westley, Brenda Zimmerman, and Michael Quinn Patton** (2007) Getting to Maybe: How the World is Changed. Excerpt: http://tinyurl.com/q6bcsbx

Also consider: **C.S. (Buzz) Holling and Lance Gunderson (eds.)** (2002) Panarchy: Understanding Transformations in Human and Natural Systems.

Bob Williams and Richard Hummelbrunner (2010) Systems Concepts in Action: A Practitioner's Toolkit. Excerpts: http://tinyurl.com/q2qxfyo

Anna Birney (2014) Cultivating System Change: A Practitioner's Companion. http://tinyurl.com/qjxk4eb

Classic publication: **Donella Meadows** (1999) Leverage Points: Places to Intervene in a System http://donellameadows.org/wp-content/userfiles/Leverage_Points.pdf

PRINCIPLE 2: Transform institutions

Top reading: **Jim Woodhill** (2008) Shaping Behaviour: How Institutions Evolve. www.thebrokeronline.eu/Articles/Shaping-behaviour

Also consider: **Frances Cleaver** (2012) Development Through Bricolage: Rethinking Institutions for Natural Resource Management.

Jaime Faustino and David Booth (2014) Development Entrepreneurship: How Donors and Leaders can Foster Institutional Change. ODI/The Asia Foundation http://tinyurl.com/pm3dn8x

Jim Woodhill (2010) Capacities for Institutional Innovation: A Complexity Perspective. http://tinyurl.com/nnd65xo

Classic publication: **Elinor Ostrom** (1990) Governing the Commons: The Evolution of Institutions for Collective Action.

PRINCIPLE 3: Work with power

Top reading: **Lisa VeneKlasen with Valerie Miller** (2002) A New Weave of Power, People and Politics: The Action Guide for Advocacy and Citizen Participation.

Also consider: **Wim Hiemstra, Herman Brouwer, and Simone van Vugt** (2012) Power Dynamics in Multi-Stakeholder Processes: A Balancing Act. http://tinyurl.com/now5jl2

Raji Hunjan and Jethro Pettit (2011) Power: A Practical Guide for Facilitating Social Change. http://tinyurl.com/q3lwbna

Classic publication: **Steven Lukes** (1974) Power: A Radical View.

PRINCIPLE 4: Deal with conflict

Top reading: **Christopher Moore** (2014, fourth edition) The Mediation Process: A Practical Guide to Conflict Management.

Also consider: **Jean Paul Lederach** (2003) The Little Book of Conflict Transformation.

Roger Sidaway (2005) Resolving Environmental Disputes: From Conflict to Consensus.

Roger Fisher and William Ury (1981) Getting to Yes: How to Negotiate Agreement without Giving In. Harvard Negotiation Project.

Classic publication: **Gene Sharp** (1994; 2012). From Dictatorship to Democracy: A Conceptual Framework for Liberation.

PRINCIPLE 5: Communicate effectively

Top reading: **Andrew F. Acland** (2003) Perfect People Skills: All You Need to Get It Right First Time.

Also consider: **Marshall Rosenberg** (2003) Nonviolent Communication: A Language of Life.

Eric E. Vogt, Juanita Brown, and David Isaacs (2003) The Art of Powerful Questions: Catalyzing Insight, Innovation, and Action. www.leveragenetworks.com

Bettye Pruitt and Philip Thomas (2007) Democratic Dialogue: A Handbook for Practitioners. http://tinyurl.com/jdxnm79

Classic publication: **William Isaacs** (1999) Dialogue and the Art of Thinking Together: A Pioneering Approach to Communicating in Business and in Life.

PRINCIPLE 6: Promote collaborative leadership

Top reading: **David Archer and Alex Cameron** (2013) Collaborative Leadership: Building Relationships, Handling Conflict and Sharing Control.

Also consider: **Adam Kahane** (2010) Power and Love: A Theory and Practice of Social Change.

Classic publication: **Barbara Gray** (1989) Collaborating: Finding Common Ground for Multiparty Problems.

PRINCIPLE 7: Foster participatory learning

Top reading: **Robert Chambers** (2002) Participatory Workshops: A Sourcebook of 21 Sets of Ideas and Activities. Also see: www.participatorymethods.org

Also consider: **Peter Senge, Bryan Smith, Richard Ross, Charlotte Roberts, and Art Kleiner** (1994) The Fifth Discipline Fieldbook: Strategies and Tools for Building a Learning Organization. Also see http://tinyurl.com/nbd95l6

The Barefoot Guide Connection (2009) The Barefoot Guide to Learning Practices in Organisations and Social Change. www.barefootguide.org

Classic publication: **David Kolb** (1984). Experiential Learning: Experience as a Source of Learning and Development

Our top websites

You can find many web sites with material relevant to the design and facilitation of MSPs. These are the ones that we have found most useful.

www.aral.com.au/arhome.html Simple descriptions of many participatory analytical tools by action research and learning expert Bob Dick

www.conflictsensitivity.org/content/how-guide Material on dealing with conflict

http://creatingminds.co.uk/tools/tools_all.htm Tools to enhance creativity, alone and in groups

http://diytoolkit.org Practical tools to trigger and support social innovation

www.grantcraft.org/tools/interactive-tool-finder A nice selection of tools for online collaboration

www.iied.org/participatory-learning-action Materials and tools to support action learning for development

www.kstoolkit.org Knowledge sharing toolkit

http://learningforsustainability.net Tools and models to support social learning and collective action around sustainability issues

www.managingforimpact.org/ A CDI-hosted portal with resources on participatory planning, monitoring, and evaluation.

www.participatorymethods.org Materials and tools to support participation

http://partnershipbrokers.org Home of Parnership Brokering Association, with resources and online journal Betwixt & Between

www.powercube.net Resources to analyse and work with power

http://seedsforchange.org.uk/resources#grp Practical guide on consensus decision making

www.theoryofchange.nl A CDI-hosted portal on theory of change

www.visual-literacy.org/periodic_table/periodic_table.html Overview of ways to visualize data

NOTES

1 INTRODUCTION

1 Austin (2000)
2 Vurro, Dacin, and Perrini (2010)
3 Huijstee, Mariette van (2012)
http://somo.nl/publications-en/
Publication_3786
4 Porter and Kramer (2011)
http://tinyurl.com/pb6eo6w

2 MULTI-STAKEHOLDER PARTNERSHIPS

5 Dentoni and Peterson (2011)
6 Pattberg and Widerberg (2014)
7 See Milder, Hart, Dobie, Minai, and Zeleski (2014) and Estrada-Carmona, Hart, DeClerck, Harvey, and Milder (2014). These studies cite "'Incomplete' or 'shallow' stakeholder engagement as the most frequently reported challenge by the nearly two hundred landscape initiatives from 54 countries (33 African and 21 from the LAC region) that participated in the studies. African initiatives were the most affected.
8 Studies (Bitzer and Glasbergen 2015; Pattberg and Widerberg 2014) suggest that MSPs often do not reach their full potential, partly due to insufficient attention to process design. This can lead, for example, to lack of participation of certain stakeholder groups, unrealistic goal setting, or lack of focus on learning and innovation.
9 World Wildlife Fund (2012)
http://tinyurl.com/pkaujac

3 DESIGNING THE PROCESS

1 Black (2014)
2 If you find this checklist useful, consider also using the extended Checklist for MSP Designers in Chapter 8 of Hemmati (2002)
3 de Man (2013)
4 http://eiti.org
5 We use the term 'meetings' in a broad sense. It can also imply workshops, gatherings, or events, though not training sessions.
6 See Flower and Muoio (2013) p. 15
www.rockefellerfoundation.org/bellagio-center/gather-art-science-effective
7 www.chathamhouse.org.uk/about/chathamhouserule/

4 SEVEN PRINCIPLES THAT MAKE MSPs EFFECTIVE

1 Waddell (2011) pp. 96–105; and Waddell (2014) The Table builds on work by David Snowden and Steve Waddell.
2 www.sustainablefoodlab.org
3 See Snowden and Boone (2007) and Kurtz and Snowden (2003).
Also: http://cognitive-edge.com
Cynefin is a Welsh word meaning roughly 'the places where you belong'. The name of the first domain, 'Obvious', was 'Simple' in previous versions of the framework (see www.en.wikipedia.org/wiki/Cynefin). Other authors have also contributed to applying complexity science to management – for example, Stacey (2012).
4 In his most recent work, Snowden has changed the name of the 'Simple' domain to 'Obvious', implying that the relationship between cause and effect is obvious to all. We continue to use the term 'Simple' to be consistent with the terminology of other models (Waddell (2010) and Westley, Zimmerman, and Patton (2007)).
5 Westley, Zimmerman, and Patton (2007), p 9.
6 See for example Checkland and Poulter (2006).
7 We follow Williams and van 't Hof (2014) in summarising systems thinking using the three concepts of inter-relationships, perspectives, and boundaries.
8 Mulgan & Leadbeater (2013), page 12.
9 www.issdethiopia.org
10 http://en.wikipedia.org/wiki/Ken_Wilber#Quadrants
11 Waddell (2011) p 106–107.
12 Walters (2014) http://tinyurl.com/o6jdz86
13 The Generative Change Community, in which the authors have been involved, is a community of practitioners that has developed change leadership tools and capacities. The Process Inquiry Protocol can be found: http://tinyurl.com/p79y2e7
14 Adapted from the original tool developed by Reos Partners (2010).
http://tinyurl.com/o7augrf
15 We follow Jones et al. (2011) and Senge (1990) in defining mental models as personal, internal representations of external reality that people use to interact with the world around them. They are constructed by individuals on the basis of their unique life experiences, perceptions, and understandings of the world. Mental models often present obstacles to learning and innovation, as they limit the ways in which we think and act.
16 For example, Hodgson (2006) and Cleaver (2012).
17 Woodhill (2010) and Woodhill (2008) Shaping Behaviour: How institutions evolve.
www.thebrokeronline.eu/Articles/Shaping-behaviour
18 Mckeown, Rozemeijer, and Wit (2013)
http://tinyurl.com/p5zvwrn
19 Batchelor (2012). This case draws upon 10 years of experience of one of the principal people involved in the development of M-PESA.
20 https://ict4dblog.wordpress.com/2012/11/24/why-m-pesa-outperforms-other-developing-country-mobile-money-schemes

21 Achi Garvey and Berger (2015) www.mckinsey.com/insights/managing_in_uncertainty/delighting_in_the_possible
22 French and Raven (1959). http://en.wikipedia.org/wiki/French_and_Raven%27s_bases_of_power
23 VeneKlasen and Miller (2002).
24 This section is adapted from www.participatorymethods.org/method/power
25 This section is partly based on www.participatorymethods.org/method/power
26 Courtesy of Partnership Brokering Association (PBA)/Ros Tennyson.
www.partnershipbrokers.org
27 Source: personal communication Henk Zingstra (Wageningen UR, CDI) and OECD (2008:123) http://tinyurl.com/p5zd8ry
28 On using conflict for positive outcomes, see Margaret Heffernan's TED talk Dare to Disagree http://tinyurl.com/pfxjn93
29 Zeldin (1998)
30 Isaacs (1999) p 41.
31 Isaacs (1999)
32 www.cnvc.org is based in San Francisco but works with certified trainers in NVC worldwide. These concepts may already help you to obtain insights, but practising them is less easy. Follow the open trainings agenda on the CNVC website for opportunities in your area.
33 Taken from www.nonviolentcommunication.com/freeresources/nvc_social_media_quotes.htm
34 Vogt, Brown and Isaacs (2003)
Also: www.leveragenetworks.com
35 Cain (2012) and www.thepowerofintroverts.com
36 See www.belbin.com for background on the nine team roles and commercially available tests.
37 More information, including tests you can take to find out which roles you naturally fulfil, at www.belbin.com
38 Kahane (2010). Also see this 30 minute talk of Adam Kahane for the Royal Society of Arts.
39 Paul Tillich regarded love, power and justice as categories of being, whereby 'justice preserves what love unites' (Tillich (1954)).
40 Senge, Hamilton, and Kania (2015): The dawn of system leadership.
41 www.mspguide.org/tool/preferred-learning-styles
42 Argyris and Schon (1974 and 1978).
43 If you are interested in how to monitor and evaluate the learning within your MSP, we recommend the work of Etienne and Beverly Wenger-Trayner on assessing value creation in networks and communities of practice. For example http://wenger-trayner.com/resources/publications/evaluation-framework/

5 FROM DESIGN TO PRACTICE

1 Mann (2007) http://tinyurl.com/p46sgwz
2 Manning and Roessler (2014).
3 Fowler (2014) http://repub.eur.nl/pub/51129
4 Swaans et al. (2013).
5 Sørensen and Torfing (2013)
http://tinyurl.com/nzadmnk

6 This paragraph is based on Hemmati (2010), pp. 12–13

7 For a comprehensive introduction to Action Research see Chevalier and Buckles (2013). Or access www.aral.com.au, our first place to start on Action Research & Action Learning.

8 Manring (2007).

9 As explained by, for example, Thomas and Inkson (2009). Also see GLOBE (Global Leadership and Organizational Behavior Effectiveness Research: http://tinyurl.com/nwoz4ee), which studied differences in culture in 62 countries, based on Hofstede's classic work in this area (1980).

10 Hemmati (2010).

11 Scharmer and Kaufer (2013).

12 Other explanations of how individual commitment develops are by looking at the right incentive systems (cognitive psychology) and by not fearing change (psychoanalytical point of view).

13 Senge, Hamilton, and Kania (2015) www.ssireview.org/articles/entry/the_dawn_of_system_leadership

14 Kahneman (2011) http://en.wikipedia.org/wiki/Thinking,_Fast_and_Slow

15 Enayati (2002).

16 Three examples: (1) Surowiecki (2005); (2) Haslam (2001); (3) Dörner (1997).

17 The importance of support structures is illustrated in a review of backbone organisations in collective impact by Turner et al. (2012).

18 Tennyson (2003) http://thepartneringinitiative.org/publications/toolbook-series/the-partnering-toolbook/ (requires registration).

19 Ibid., p. 13.

20 Hemmati (2002), p. 224.

21 McManus and Tennyson (2008). http://thepartneringinitiative.org/publications/toolbook-series/talking-the-walk/

22 Chatham House Rule: http://www.chathamhouse.org/about/chatham-house-rule

6 CHOOSING TOOLS

1 See Salomon and Engel (1997) and the RAAKS dossier of the Bibliotheca Alexandrina: KIT Dossier RAAKS: multi-stakeholder learning in agricultural innovation systems. http://tinyurl.com/njfeb4b

2 See, for example, www.openspaceworld.org, www.futuresearch.net, and https://appreciativeinquiry.case.edu

3 www.ideo.com and www.ideo.com/by-ideo/human-centered-design-toolkit

4 www.nesta.org.uk and the Development, Impact, and You Toolkit http://diytoolkit.org.

5 Social Innovation Generation (Canada): www.sigeneration.ca

6 www.idea.int/publications/democratic_dialogue http://dialogos.com, or http://ncdd.org

7 Kaner (2014)

8 http://www.rockefellerfoundation.org/bellagio-center/gather-art-science-effective

9 The six purposes are consistent with Kolb's experiential learning cycle (Section 4, Principle 7). The learning styles developed by Kolb indicate that some people are competent in divergent learning and others in convergent learning. Different types of learners flourish at different stages of a process.

10 See http://www.wageningenportals.nl/msp/tool/rich-picture

11 Courtesy of NESTA DIY Toolkit (2014) http://diytoolkit.org, tool #8.

12 Developed by Eva Schiffer/IFPRI. See https://netmap.wordpress.com/ and http://en.wikipedia.org/wiki/Net-map_toolbox

13 We present a light version of World Café. You can find variations and further resources on http://www.theworldcafe.com/method.html.

14 Developed by Dave Snowden/Cognitive Edge. See http://en.wikipedia.org/wiki/Cynefin and http://cognitive-edge.com

15 Developed by Ken Wilber. See http://en.wikipedia.org/wiki/Ken_Wilber#Quadrants

16 Developed by John Gaventa and team (IDS Sussex). www.powercube.net/analyse-power/forms-of-power/ and www.participatorymethods.org/method/power

17 Adapted from original concept of Edward De Bono. www.debonogroup.com/six_thinking_hats.php and http://en.wikipedia.org/wiki/Six_Thinking_Hats

18 Courtesy of Senge (1994), p. 273.

19 Developed by Leon de Caluwé and Hans Vermaak, both TwynstraGudde advisors. See de Caluwé and Vermaak (2002) and www.toolshero.com/colour-thinking-caluwe-vermaak/
The test can be accessed for free at http://hansvermaak.com/blog/publicaties/the-color-test-for-change-agents/

20 Developed by Meredith Belbin. www.belbin.com

21 The Conflict Style test was developed by Kenneth Thomas and Ralph Kilmann. www.kilmanndiagnostics.com/catalog/thomas-kilmann-conflict-mode-instrument

22 Tennyson (2003) http://thepartneringinitiative.org/publications/toolbook-series/the-partnering-toolbook/ (requires registration).

23 Developed by Eelke Wielinga. www.linkconsult.nl/files/Circle-of-Coherence-Description.pdf

24 Courtesy of IDEO's Human-Centered Design Toolkit (2011–2015) www.designkit.org.

25 Adapted from Thomas and Pruitt (2009), p. 131, based on the tool Study Guides from NIF National Issues Forum. www.idea.int/publications/democratic_dialogue/

26 Developed by Dave Snowden/Cognitive Edge. http://cognitive-edge.com/basic-methods/ritual-dessent/

27 Kaner et al. (2014), p. 267–268.

28 CDI's Reflection Booklet (2015) can be downloaded from www.wageningenUR.nl/cdi

29 Developed by Bob Dick (1984, adaptation: Bob Williams) www.bobwilliams.co.nz/Tools_files/half.pdf

7 MSPs IN ACTION

1 www.growasia.org

2 Shell has a joint venture in Nigeria called SPDC, the Shell Petroleum Development Company. SPDC owns the pipeline. Shell has a 30% share in SPDC, the Nigerian government 55%.

3 For example, www.theguardian.com/environment/2015/jan/07/shell-announces-55m-payout-for-nigeria-oil-spills

4 A visual of this framework can be found at www.ecologyandsociety.org/vol13/iss2/art34/figure2.html.

5 www.wageningenur.nl/en/show/CDIcourse_competing_claims_2015.htm.

6 See for, example, Giller et al. (2009): http://www.ecologyandsociety.org/vol13/iss2/art34.

8 ADDITIONAL RESOURCES

1 Beck (1995, 1997, 1999)

2 Offe (1996)

3 Held (1989)

4 Dryzek (1997)

5 Giddens (1998)

6 Habermas (1984)

7 Holling and Gunderson (2002)

8 For example, Kurtz and Snowden (2003), Snowden and Boone (2007), or www.cognitive-edge.com

9 Ramalingan (2013) and http://aidontheedge.info

10 Zolli (2012)

11 Westley (2013) and Westley, Zimmerman, and Patton (2007)

12 Harford (2012)

13 Beinhocker (2007)

14 Kahneman (2011)

14 Dolan et al. (2011); World Development Report 2015. http://www.worldbank.org/en/publication/wdr2015

16 Enayati (2002)

17 Institute for Government, Cabinet Office (2010)

18 Such as Thaler and Sunstein (2008)

19 World Development Report 2015 http://www.worldbank.org/en/publication/wdr2015

20 Geels and Schot (2007)

21 Blok (2014)

22 For example, www.rsm.nl/people/jan-rotmans or Grin, Rotmans, and Schot (2012)

23 van Paassen et al. (2014), Klerkx et al. (2012), and Pyburn and Woodhill (2014)

24 Austin (2000)

25 Gray (1989, 2013)

26 Glasbergen, Biermann, and Mol (eds.) (2007)

27 Waddell (2011)

28 Termeer; Dewulf, Breeman, and Stiller (2013)

29 Termeer et al. (2012), Williams and Van 't Hoff (2014)

30 Bitzer and Glasbergen (2015)

REFERENCES

Achi, Zafer and Jennifer Garvey Berger (2015) Delighting in the possible. McKinsey Quarterly, March 2015 issue. www.mckinsey.com/insights/managing_in_uncertainty/delighting_in_the_possible

...

Acland, Andrew F (2003, revised edition) Perfect People Skills: All You Need to Get it Right First Time. London: Random House Business Books.

...

ActionAid (2012) Power: Elite Capture and Hidden influence. http://tinyurl.com/ots9ace

...

Archer, David and Alex Cameron (2013) Collaborative Leadership: Building Relationships, Handling Conflict and Sharing Control. London: Routledge.

...

Argyris, Chris and Donald Schön (1978) Organizational Learning: A Theory of Action Perspective. Reading, MA: Addison-Wesley.

...

Argyris, Chris and Donald Schön (1974) Theory in Practice: Increasing Professional Effectiveness. San Francisco: Jossey-Bass.

...

Austin, James (2000) The Collaboration Challenge: How Nonprofits and Business Succeed through Strategic Alliances. San Francisco: Jossey-Bass.

...

Austin, James and May Seitanidi (2012) Collaborative value creation: A review of partnering between nonprofits and businesses. Part I. Value creation spectrum and collaboration stages. Nonprofit and Voluntary Sector Quarterly, 41(5) 726–758.

...

Barefoot Guide Connection (2009) The Barefoot Guide to Learning Practices in Organisations and Social Change. www.barefootguide.org

...

Batchelor, Simon (2012) Changing the financial landscape of Africa: An unusual story of evidence-informed innovation, intentional policy influence and private sector engagement. IDS Bulletin, Vol. 43, Issue 5, pp. 84–90. http://tinyurl.com/of3ho38

...

Beck, Ulrich (1999) World Risk Society. Cambridge: Polity Press

...

Beck, Ulrich (1995) Ecological Politics in an Age of Risk. Cambridge: Polity Press.

...

Beck, Ulrich (1997) The Reinvention of Politics: Rethinking Modernity in the Global Social Order. Cambridge: Polity Press.

...

Beinhocker, Eric (2007) The Origin of Wealth: Evolution, Complexity and The Radical Remaking of Economics. London: Random House Business.

...

Birney, Anna (2014) Cultivating System Change: A Practitioner's Companion. Oxford: DoSustainability. http://tinyurl.com/qjxk4eb

...

Bitzer, Verena and Pieter Glasbergen (2015) Business–NGO partnerships in global value chains: part of the solution or part of the problem of sustainable change? Current Opinion in Environmental Sustainability, 12:35–40

...

Black, Liam (2014) The social entrepreneur's A to Z. London: London Fields Publishing.

...

Blok, Vincent (2014): Look who's talking: responsible innovation, the paradox of dialogue and the voice of the other in communication and negotiation processes. Journal of Responsible Innovation, Vol. 1, Issue 2.

...

Brouwer, Herman, Annemarie Groot Kormelinck and Simone van Vugt (2012) Tools for Analysing Power in Multi-Stakeholder Processes. Wageningen UR, CDI. http://tinyurl.com/pqe99jr

...

Cain, Susan (2012) Quiet: The Power of Introverts in a World that Can't Stop Talking. London: Penguin/Viking.

...

de Caluwé, L. and H. Vermaak (2002) Learning to Change: A Guide for Organizational Change Agents. Thousand Oaks, CA: Sage.

...

Chambers, Robert (2002) Participatory Workshops: A Sourcebook of 21 Sets of Ideas and Activities. London: Earthscan.

...

Checkland, Peter and Jim Scholes (1999) Soft Systems Methodology in Action. London: Wiley.

...

Checkland, Peter B. and Poulter, J (2006) Learning for Action: A Short Definitive Account of Soft Systems Methodology and its Use for Practitioners, Teachers and Students. Chichester, UK: Wiley.

...

Chevalier, Jacques and Daniel Buckles (2013) Participatory Action Research: Theory and Methods for Engaged Inquiry. London: Routledge.

...

Cleaver, Frances (2012) Development through Bricolage: Rethinking Institutions for Natural Resource Management. London: Earthscan.

...

Dentoni, Domenico and H. Christopher Peterson (2011) Multi-stakeholder sustainability alliances in agri-food chains: a framework for multi-disciplinary research. International Food and Agribusiness Management Review, Vol. 14, Issue 5, pp. 83–108.

...

Dolan, Paul, Michael Hallsworth, David Halpern, Dominique King, Robert Metcalfe and Ivo Vlaev (2011) Influencing behaviour: The mindspace way. Journal of Economic Psychology 33 (2012) 264–277

...

Dörner, Dietrich (1997) The Logic of Failure. Recognizing and Avoiding Error in Complex Situations. New York: Metropolitian Books.

...

Dryzek, John (1997) The Politics of the Earth: Environmental Discourses. Oxford: Oxford University Press.

...

Enayati, Jasmin (2002) Effective communication and decision making in diverse groups. In: Minu Hemmati, Multi-Stakeholder Processes for Governance and Sustainability: Beyond Deadlock and Conflict. London: Earthscan, pp.73–95.

...

Estrada-Carmona, Natalia, Abigail Hart, Fabrice DeClerck, Celia Harvey and Jeffrey Milder (2014) Integrated landscape management for agriculture, rural livelihoods, and ecosystem conservation: An assessment of experience from Latin America and the Caribbean. Landscape and Urban Planning 129:1–11

...

Faustino, Jaime and David Booth (2014) Development Entrepreneurship: How Donors and Leaders can Foster Institutional Change. ODI/The Asia Foundation http://tinyurl.com/pm3dn8x

...

French, John and Bertrand Raven (1959) The bases of social power. In Studies in Social Power, D. Cartwright (ed.), pp. 150–167. Ann Arbor, MI: Institute for Social Research. Summary: http://tinyurl.com/nfk48cc

...

Fisher, Roger and William Ury (1981) Getting to Yes: How to Negotiate Agreement without Giving In. Harvard Negotiation Project

...

Flower, Noah Rimland and Anna Muoio (2013) GATHER: The Art and Science of Effective Convening. Monitor Institute/Deloitte & Rockefeller Foundation http://www.rockefellerfoundation.org/bellagio-center/gather-art-science-effective

...

Fowler, Alan (2014) Innovation in Institutional Collaboration: The Role of Interlocutors. Institute of Social Studies, The Hague. Civil Collaboration Research Initiative Working paper No. 3. http://repub.eur.nl/pub/51129

...

Geels, Frank and Johan Schot (2007) Typology of sociotechnical transition pathways. Research Policy 36, pp. 399–417.

...

Generative Change Community (2007) Process Inquiry Protocol. http://tinyurl.com/o79mlay

...

Gharajedaghi, Jamshid (1999) Systems Thinking: Managing Chaos and Complexity. A Platform for Designing Business Architecture. Butterworth-Heinemann.

...

Gaventa, John (2006) Finding the Spaces for Change: A Power Analysis. IDS Bulletin, Vol. 37, No. 6. http://tinyurl.com/p7zrutm

...

Giddens, Anthony (1998) The Third Way: The Renewal of Social Democracy. Cambridge: Polity.

...

Giller, Ken; Cees Leeuwis, Jens Anderson, Wim Andriesse, Arie Brouwer, Peter Frost, Paul Hebinck, Ignas Heitkönig, Martin van Ittersum, Niek Koning, Ruerd Ruben, Maja Slingerland, Henk Udo, Tom Veldkamp, Claudius van de Vijver, Mark van Wijk and Pieter Windmeijer (2008) Competing Claims on Natural Resources: What Role for Science? Ecology & Society, Vol 13, No 2, Article 34.

...

Glasbergen, Pieter, Frank Biermann and Arthur Mol (eds.) (2007) Partnerships, Governance and Sustainable Development: Reflections on Theory And Practice. Cheltenham, UK and Northampton, MA: Edward Elgar. http://tinyurl.com/nkbslk3

...

Gray, Barbara (1989) Collaborating: Finding Common Ground for Multiparty Problems. San Francisco: Jossey-Bass

...

Gray, Barbara and Jenne P. Sites (2013) Sustainability through Partnerships: Capitalizing on Collaboration. Retrieved from: nbs.net/knowledge.
...

Grin, John, Jan Rotmans and Johan Schot (2010). Transitions to Sustainable Development. Routledge Studies in Sustainability Transitions. New York: Routledge. http://tinyurl.com/n9fe56m
...

Habermas, Jürgen (1981; 1984) Theory of Communicative Action, Volume One: Reason and the Rationalization of Society. Boston, MA: Beacon Press.
...

Harford, Tim (2012) Adapt: Why Success Always Starts with Failure. London: Picador
...

Hofstede, Geert (1980). Motivation, leadership, and organization: do American theories apply abroad? Organizational Dynamics, Summer, 42–63
...

Holling, C.S (Buzz) and Lance Gunderson (eds.) (2002) Panarchy: Understanding Transformations in Human and Natural Systems. Washington, DC: Island Press.
...

Hoppe, Rob (2010) The Governance of Problems: Puzzling, Powering, and Participation. Policy Press: Bristol
...

Haslam, Alexander (2001) Psychology in Organizations: The Social Identity Approach. London: Sage.
...

Hart, Stuart and Sharma, Sanjay (2004) Engaging fringe stakeholders for competitive imagination. Academy of Management Executive, Vol. 18, No 1.
...

Held, David (1989). Political Theory and the Modern State: Essays on State, Power, and Democracy. Stanford, CA: Stanford University Press.
...

Hemmati, Minu (2002) Multi-Stakeholder Processes for Governance and Sustainability: Beyond Deadlock and Conflict. London: Earthscan.
...

Hemmati, Minu (2010) What it takes: competencies needed to design and facilitate MSPs. Capacity.org, Issue 41 on Facilitating Multi-Actor Change, December 2010. http://tinyurl.com/qzto7ca
...

Hiemstra, Wim, Herman Brouwer and Simone van Vugt (2012) Power Dynamics in Multi-Stakeholder Processes: A Balancing Act. ETC Foundation/CDI, Wageningen UR. http://tinyurl.com/now5jl2
...

Hodgson, Geoffrey (2006) What are institutions? Journal of Economic Issues, XL(1).
...

Huijstee, Mariette van (2012) Multi-Stakeholder Initiatives: A Strategic Guide for Civil Society Organizations. Amsterdam: SOMO. http://somo.nl/publications-en/Publication_3786
...

Hunjan, Raji and Pettit, Jethro 2011. Power: A Practical Guide for Facilitating Social Change. Carnegie Trust/IDS, UK. http://tinyurl.com/q3lwbna
...

IDEO (2011–2015) Human Centred Design Toolkit. San Francisco: IDEO. www.designkit.org (requires registration)
...

Institute for Government, Cabinets Office (2010) MINDSPACE: Influencing Behaviour Through Public Policy. www.instituteforgovernment.org.uk/publications/mindspace
...

Isaacs, William (1999) Dialogue and the Art of Thinking Together: A Pioneering Approach to Communicating in Business and in Life. New York: Doubleday.
...

Jenkins, Jon and Maureen Jenkins (2006) The 9 Disciplines of a Facilitator: Leading Groups by Transforming Yourself. International Association of Facilitators (IAF). San Francisco: Jossey-Bass
...

Jones, Nathalie, Helen Ross, Timothy Lynam, Pascal Perez and Anne Leitch (2011) Mental models: an interdisciplinary synthesis of theory and methods. Ecology and Society, Vol. 16(1): 46. http://tinyurl.com/nlgycun
...

Kahane, Adam (2004) Solving Tough Problems: An Open Way of Talking, Listening, and Creating New Realities. San Francisco: Berrett-Kohler.
...

Kahane, Adam (2010) Power and Love: A Theory and Practice of Social Change. San Francisco: Reos/Berrett-Koehler.
...

Kahneman, Daniel (2011) Thinking, fast and Slow, New York: Farrar, Straus and Giroux. http://en.wikipedia.org/wiki/Thinking,_Fast_and_Slow
...

Kaner, Sam, Lenny Lind, Catherine Toldi, Sarah Fisk and Duane Berger (2014, third edition) Facilitator's Guide to Participatory Decision-Making. San Francisco: Jossey-Bass.
...

Kania, John, Mark Kramer, et al (2011–2015) A series of articles on collective impact for Stanford Social Innovation Review: www.ssireview.org/articles/entry/collective_impact
...

KIT, Agri-ProFocus and IIRR (2012) Challenging Chains to Change: Gender Equity in Agricultural Value Chain Development. Amsterdam: KIT Publishers, Royal Tropical Institute. www.kit.nl/gender/wp-content/uploads/publications/2008_chachacha.pdf
...

Klerkx, Laurens, Barbara van Mierlo and Cees Leeuwis (2012) Evolution of systems approaches to agricultural innovation: concepts, analysis and interventions. In: I. Darnhofer, D. Gibbon and B. Dedieu (eds.), Farming Systems Research into the 21st Century: The New Dynamic. Dordrecht: Springer Science/Business Media.
...

Kolb, David (1984). Experiential Learning: Experience as a Source of Learning and Development. New Jersey: Prentice Hall.
...

Kupers, Roland (2014, editor) Turbulence: a corporate perspective on collaborating for resilience. Amsterdam: Amsterdam University Press.
...

Kurtz, Cynthia and David Snowden (2003) The new dynamics of strategy: Sense-making in a complex and complicated world. IBM Systems Journal Vol. 42, No. 3, p. 462–483.
...

Lederach, Jean Paul (2003) The Little Book of Conflict Transformation. Intercourse, PA: Good Books. Excerpt: http://tinyurl.com/nvp3s5y
...

Lukes, Steven (1974) Power: A Radical View. London: Macmillan Press
...

Man, Ard-Pieter de (2013) Alliances: an Executive Guide to Designing Successful Strategic Partnerships. Chichester, UK: Wiley.
...

Mann, Tony (2007) Facilitation: an Art, Science, Skill or All Three? http://resourceproductions.com/books/facilitation-art-science-skill-or-all-three
...

Manning, Stephan and Daniel Roessler (2014) The formation of cross-sector development partnerships: How bridging agents shape project agendas and longer-term alliances. Journal of Business Ethics 123:527–547
...

Manring, Susan 2007. Creating and managing inter-organizational learning networks to achieve sustainable ecosystem management. Organization & Environment, 20(3): 325–346.
...

Mckeown, James Parker, Nico Rozemeijer and Marieke Wit (2013) The Multi-Stakeholder Dialogue in Ghana: Towards A Negotiated Solution to Illegal Chainsaw Milling. Wageningen/Accra: Tropenbos. http://tinyurl.com/pf7epjl
...

McManus, Sue and Ros Tennyson (2008) Talking the Walk: A Communication Manual for Partnership Practitioners. IBLF/The Partnering Initiative. http://tinyurl.com/os2p2pk (requires registration).
...

Meadows, Donella (1999) Leverage Points: Places to Intervene in a System. The Sustainability Institute. www.thesolutionsjournal.com/node/419
...

Milder, Jeffrey, Abigail Hart, Philip Dobie, Joshua Minai, Christi Zaleski (2014) Integrated landscape initiatives for African agriculture, development, and conservation: A region-wide assessment. World Development, Vol. 54, pp. 68–80.
...

Moore, Christopher (2014, fourth edition) The Mediation Process: A Practical Guide to Conflict Management. San Francisco: Jossey-Bass.
...

Mulgan, Geoff and Charlie Leadbeater (2013) System Innovation: Discussion Paper. London: NESTA. www.nesta.org.uk/publications/systems-innovation-discussion-paper.
...

OECD (2008) OECD rural policy reviews: Netherlands. Paris: OECD. http://tinyurl.com/p5zd8ry
...

Offe, Claus (1996) Modernity and the State: East, West. Cambridge: Polity Press.
...

Ostrom, Elinor (1990) Governing the Commons: The Evolution of Institutions for Collective Action. Cambridge, UK and New York: Cambridge University Press
...

Paassen, Annemarie van, Laurens Klerkx, Richard Adu-Acheampong, Samuel Adjei-Nsiah and Elisabeth Zannoue (2014) Agricultural innovation platforms in West Africa: How does strategic institutional entrepreneurship unfold in different value chain contexts? Outlook on AGRICULTURE, Vol. 43, No. 3, 2014, pp. 193–200.
…

Pattberg, Philipp and Oscar Widerberg (2014): Transnational Multi-Stakeholder Partnerships for Sustainable Development: Building Blocks for Success. IVM Report, R-14/31. Amsterdam: Institute for Environmental Studies. https://icscentre.org/area/multi-stakeholder-partnerships
…

Porter, Michael and Mark Kramer (2011) Creating shared value. Harvard Business Review, January–February. https://hbr.org/2011/01/the-big-idea-creating-shared-value
…

Pretty, Jules, Irene Guijt, Ian Scoones and John Thompson (1995) Participatory Learning and Action: A Trainer's Guide. London: IIED http://pubs.iied.org/6021IIED.html
…

Pruitt, Bettye and Philip Thomas (2007) Democratic Dialogue: A Handbook for Practitioners. Washington, DC: CIDA, International IDEA, the GS/OAS and UNDP. http://tinyurl.com/nv8cafr
…

Pyburn, Rhiannon and Jim Woodhill (2015) Dynamics of Innovation: Primer for Emerging Professionals. KIT/CDI, LM Publishers. http://tinyurl.com/nn87b5h
…

Ramalingam, Ben (2013) Aid on the Edge of Chaos. Oxford: Oxford University Press.
…

Rosenberg, Marshall (2003) Nonviolent Communication: A Language of Life. Puddledancer Press.
…

Scharmer, Otto and Katrin Kaufer (2013) Leading from the Emerging Future. San Francisco: Berrett-Koehler. http://tinyurl.com/loje74j
…

Senge, Peter, Bryan Smith, Richard Ross, Charlotte Roberts and Art Kleiner (1994) The Fifth Discipline Fieldbook: Strategies and Tools for Building a Learning Organization. Crown Business Publishers. Also see http://tinyurl.com/nbd95l6
…

Senge, Peter, Hal Hamilton and John Kania (2015) The dawn of system leadership. Stanford Social Innovation Review, Winter issue. www.ssireview.org/articles/entry/the_dawn_of_system_leadership
…

Sharp, Gene (1994; 2012). From Dictatorship to Democracy: A Conceptual Framework for Liberation. London: Serpent's Tail.
…

Sidaway, Roger (2005) Resolving Environmental Disputes: From Conflict to Consensus. London: Earthscan.
…

Sloan, Pamela and David Oliver (2013) Building trust in multi-stakeholder partnerships: critical emotional incidents and practices of engagement. Organizational Studies 34(12) 1835–1868.
…

Snowden, Dave and Mary Boone (2007) A Leader's Framework for Decision Making. Harvard Business Review, November issue. http://tinyurl.com/neslybs
…

Solomon, Monique and Paul Engel (1997) Facilitating Innovation for Development: A RAAKS Resource Toolbox. KIT/CTA/STOAS. http://tinyurl.com/o58hjba
…

Sørensen, Eva and Jacob Torfing (2013) Enhancing Social Innovation by Rethinking Collaboration, Leadership and Public Governance. Paper presented at NESTA Social Frontiers, London, UK. http://tinyurl.com/namfvdc
…

Stacey, Ralph (2012) The Tools and Techniques of Leadership and Management: Meeting the Challenge of Complexity. Routledge, London.
…

Surowiecki, James (2005) The Wisdom of Crowds: Why the Many are Smarter than the Few and How Collective Wisdom Shapes Business, Economies, Societies and Nations. New York: Anchor.
…

Swaans, K., B. Cullen, A. van Rooyen, A. Adekunle, H. Ngwenya, Z. Lema and S. Nederlof (2013). Dealing with critical challenges in African innovation platforms: lessons for facilitation. Knowledge Management for Development Journal 9(3): 116–135. http://journal.km4dev.org/
…

Tennyson, Ros (2003) The Partnering Toolbook. IBLF/GAIN, p. 17. http://tinyurl.com/osgbbpb (requires registration).
…

Tennyson, Ros (2003) The Brokering guidebook: navigating partnerships for sustainable development. http://tinyurl.com/pw5bm6s
…

Termeer, Catrien, Art Dewulf, Gerard Breeman and Sabina Stiller (2013) Governance capabilities for dealing wisely with wicked problems. Administration & Society 6 January 2013, p. 1–31.
…

Thaler, Richard and Cass Sunstein (2008) Nudge: Improving Decisions about Health, Wealth and Happiness. London: Penguin.
…

Thomas, David C. and Kerr Inkson (2009, second edition) Cultural Intelligence: Living and Working Globally. San Francisco: Berrett-Koehler.
…

Tillich, Paul (1954) Love, Power and Justice: Ontological Analysis and Ethical Applications. Oxford: Oxford University Press.
…

Turner, Shiloh, Kathy Merchant, John Kania and Ellen Martin (2012) Understanding the Value of Backbone Organizations in Collective Impact 1. Stanford Social Innovation Review: http://tinyurl.com/bstkz4n
…

Vermeulen, Sonja; Jim Woodhill, Felicity Proctor, and Rik Delnoye (2008) Chain-wide learning for inclusive agrifood market development: a guide to multi-stakeholder processes for linking small-scale producers to modern markets. Wageningen: Wageningen International/IIED. http://tinyurl.com/n9g75jz
…

VeneKlasen, Lisa with Valerie Miller (2002) A New Weave of Power, People & Politics: The Action Guide for Advocacy and Citizen Participation. Oklahoma City, World Neighbors.
…

Vogt, Eric, Juanita Brown and David Isaacs (2003) The Art of Powerful Questions: Catalyzing Insight, Innovation, and Action. www.leveragenetworks.com
…

Vurro, Clodia, Tina Dacin and Francesco Perrini (2010) Institutional antecedents of partnering for social change: how institutional logics shape cross-sector social partnerships. Journal of Business Ethics, 94(1): 39–53.
…

Waddell, Steve (2011) Global Action Networks: Creating Our Future Together. New York/London: Palgrave Macmillan/Bocconi University Press.
…

Waddell, Steve (2014). Addressing the World's Critical Issues as Complex Change Challenges: The State-Of-The-Field. World Bank and GOLDEN Ecosystems Labs.
…

Walters, Hettie (2014) Changing our ways: making sense of complex multi-stakeholder systems change by using the four quadrant model. Knowledge Management for Development Journal, Vol. 9, No. 3 p. 153–166. http://tinyurl.com/o6jdz86
…

Wals, Arjen (2007) Social Learning towards a Sustainable World. Wageningen Academic Publishers. http://tinyurl.com/o2gzt32
…

Williams, Bob and Hummelbrunner, Richard (2010) System Concepts in Action: A Practitioner's Primer. Stanford, CA: Stanford University Press. Introduction: www.sup.org/books/title/?id=18331
…

Westley, Frances, Zimmerman, Brenda, Patton, and Michael Quinn (2007) Getting to Maybe: How the World is Changed. Canada: Vintage.
…

Westley, Frances (2013) Social innovation and resilience: how one enhances the other. Stanford Social Innovation Review Summer 2013. http://tinyurl.com/c6he9v6
…

Wilber, Ken (2000) A brief history of everything. Revised edition. Boulder, Colorado: Shambala Publishing
…

Woodhill, Jim (2008) Shaping behaviour: how institutions evolve. The Broker Online. www.thebrokeronline.eu/Articles/Shaping-behaviour
…

Woodhill, Jim (2010) Capacities for institutional innovation: a complexity perspective. IDS Bulletin Special Issue: Reflecting Collectively on Capacities for Change, Vol. 41, Issue 3, pp. 47–59, May 2010. http://tinyurl.com/nnd65xo
…

World Bank. 2015. World Development Report 2015: Mind, Society, and Behavior. Washington, DC: World Bank. www.worldbank.org/en/publication/wdr2015
…

World Wildlife Fund (2012) Profitability and Sustainability in Palm Oil Production: Analysis of Incremental Financial Costs and Benefits Of RSPO Compliance. http://tinyurl.com/pkaujac
…

Zeldin, Theodore (1998) Conversation: How Talk can Change Your Life. London: The Harvill Press.
…

Zolli, Andrew, Ann Marie Healy (2012) Resilience: Why Things Bounce Back. London: Headline Publishing.
…